D1405527

LEARN TO
Balance
Your Life

**a practical guide
to having it all**

MICHAEL HINZ, PH.D., AND JESSICA HINZ, PH.D.

CHRONICLE BOOKS

SAN FRANCISCO

First published in the United States in 2004 by Chronicle Books, LLC.

Conceived, created, and designed by Duncan Baird Publishers.

Library of Congress Cataloging-in-Publication Data available.

ISBN 0-8118-4301-7

Manufactured in Singapore
Typeset in Joanna MT

Managing Editors: Judy Barratt and Julia Charles
Managing Designer: Dan Sturges
Commissioned color artwork: Sandra Dionisi

Distributed in Canada by Raincoast Books
9050 Shaughnessy Street
Vancouver, British Columbia V6P 6E5

10 9 8 7 6 5 4 3 2 1

Chronicle Books LLC
85 Second Street
San Francisco, California 94105

www.chroniclebooks.com

This book is dedicated to anyone who seeks to live a great, balanced life and is ready to take charge of their destiny to make it happen.
Also, to our children, Alex and Erica, who we hope will benefit from our efforts to maintain balance within our own lives.

Contents

Introduction by Michael Hinz

Jessica and I have spent most of our careers helping others to improve their lives. Typically, these individuals have been used to making steady progress, but at a certain point they find themselves becalmed. That's when they come to us. While many people are good at learning from the past, fewer spend much time looking into the future and its unknown possibilities. They travel a certain course, passing the markers they expect to see on the way, but unaware of alternative routes that might potentially change their lives for the better forever.

The same was true of myself. Even while I was busily helping others to change their lives, I was ignoring my own. For most of us, it's far easier to tell others what they need to do than to practice what we profess. We see someone else's life situation with far greater clarity than we do our own. Like most people, I blindly followed my path, assuming that, at some point, everything would magically fall into place. Eventually, I found myself working harder and making more money than I ever had before, and for the first time in my life, I didn't have to worry about finances. There was a problem, however: I wasn't happy. It wasn't that I worked in a terrible place, but that the philosophy and values of the company clashed with my own. I was constantly trying to reconcile those differences, but in the end I chose to leave. I gave up the comfortable salary and started working toward establishing the kind of balance in my life that matched my principles and values and made sense for me. Most people would think I must have been crazy to do such a thing, and at times I have even thought the same. Nevertheless, I have no regrets, and my life has been changing for the better.

My wife, Jessica, equates balance with focus: "When I lose focus, my whole life suffers. The surest sign for me is when I've double- or triple-booked myself and then I dread trying to figure out what to do. At other times, I do the easy little things that 'call to me' rather than something else that might be harder, but more important. My life is better when I'm actively working to make it the way I want. Maintaining my balance is a creative process that never ends."

Now we both concentrate on utilizing our talents, expertise and values in ways that we find energizing rather than draining as we strive to maintain balance in our sometimes very busy lives. We enjoy assisting others to do the same. We join them where they stand, on the threshold to a brighter and better future, and help them to take the next steps into a more balanced life. If you're ready to take that next step yourself, read on. You too can discover a life that's right for you and set yourself on the road to achieving it.

Equilibrium

Have you ever dreamed of living the perfect life? We can't promise that you'll retire at 50, or reach the pinnacle of your profession or be immune to worry, but you *can* live a life that's rich and balanced – one in which you have enough time to do the things you want to do in addition to chores such as cooking, cleaning, dealing with household paperwork, and so on; you love your job and do it well; you have fulfilling relationships with friends and family; you feel healthy and energized; and your home is a comfortable haven.

This chapter introduces you to the core skills you'll need to realize your dream of a balanced life. You'll learn how to define your life vision, set your priorities and deploy your time accordingly. You'll also discover how to assess the current balance of your life and track your progress as you seek equilibrium.

What is a balanced life?

Some days you go to work and feel utterly incapable of properly completing even the simplest aspect of your job. You feel exhausted, dejected and dwarfed by the enormity of the tasks facing you. You bring these emotions home with you when you finally leave your workplace, late, having spent most of the day trying to will yourself into action. At home, every little thing seems to accuse you – dirt on the carpet, piles of unsorted paperwork in the living room, yesterday's dirty dishes spread across the kitchen worktop. Yet you're too tired and listless to do anything about them. Instead you order a pizza, open a bottle of wine and slump on the couch in front of the TV. Some time after midnight you go to bed, but your sleep is fitful at best, and you wake up the next morning filled with dread. Your life is out of balance. All of the elements of your life – work, home, health, and everything else – are conspiring to drain you of energy, motivation and satisfaction.

At other times, everything seems to fall into place. You find your job stimulating without being overwhelming. You come home at a reasonable hour, giving yourself time to unwind; you prepare a nutritious meal with fresh ingredients, over which you consider the events of the day or discuss them with your partner or a friend; and you plan what you'll do at the weekend. Perhaps you make social arrangements or you

decide to tackle a home improvement job. Later, you might relax by pursuing a hobby or by reading a book, before going to bed for a refreshing night's sleep.

Balanced living is self-perpetuating – the positive things you do in one sector of your life spread into other areas. For example, if you look after your health by eating well and exercising regularly, you'll sleep better, work more efficiently and just generally feel on top of things.

However, for many of us, this sense of balance is fleeting. All it takes is for one element to come loose and the whole structure wobbles. Perhaps a spell of hot weather disrupts your sleep, making you feel grouchy and unproductive at work and at home. Or you procrastinate over returning a friend's phone call, so that what should have been a simple conversation mutates into an imposing obstacle – a source of stressful guilt, which gnaws away at you every time you think about it.

In this book, we aim to help you create a solid structure for your life, built on firm foundations, so that the things that currently unbalance you either don't arise or, if they do, aren't allowed to unsettle you for long. At the heart of a balanced life is a clear vision (see pp.18–21) of what's most important to you and what you want to achieve.

When you take a good look at the way you're living, you may be surprised to find that you're devoting a disproportionate amount of time and effort to issues that are important to someone else, but have little value for you. Perhaps you're working all hours chasing performance targets and worrying about them while you're at home, causing your health and family life to suffer. Understanding what really matters to you helps you to set priorities and devise objectives to reflect them.

Balance goes hand in hand with organization. This may not sound particularly exciting, but through clear-sighted management of the fundamentals of your life, such as your health, your finances and your home, you can liberate yourself to pursue the things that *do* excite you.  It's a question of establishing systems to keep your life ticking over – for example, an annual medical, a weekly financial review, a daily tidy-up. Once these routines are in place, and they become second nature to you, you'll find that you take care of issues before they get out of hand, rather than letting them escalate into sources of stress and dissatisfaction that undermine your well-being.

Achieving balance may take some time, especially if you decide that you need to make a major change to your life, such as finding a new job or moving house. However, you won't necessarily need to be radical – just tweaking your existing routine can yield great benefits. You might schedule some exercise sessions every week or make a point of blitzing your housework every Saturday morning to set yourself up for a happy weekend – anything that makes you feel that you're gaining a measure of control over your life.

Often we see ways in which we can improve things, but when it comes to actually taking the necessary first steps, we can't move. We may berate ourselves for laziness, but it's rarely as simple as that. Change can be frightening, and familiarity is comforting. So, for example, you stay for years in a job that you no longer find challenging, because you get on well with your co-workers and you're afraid that you won't be able to find a more rewarding job elsewhere.

Another self-imposed obstacle to improving your life may be the feeling that to spend time, money and thought on yourself would be selfish. How can you justify such self-indulgence, you think, when there are other people to worry about? However, by shaping your life in a way that brings you happiness and fulfillment, you make yourself stronger and better able to attend to the needs of the people you care for. Priorities that seem to conflict often coincide.

Balanced living in the 21st century

The modern world places great emphasis on personal choice. In an average day we all make countless decisions – there's a range of products for every need, a computer command for every circumstance, a sandwich filling for every palate. All this gives us unprecedented opportunities to shape our lives in lots of small ways. However, having to make so many choices, often with little or no time in which to consider them, can become overwhelming. How do you decide which options will enhance, rather than detract from, the balance of your life?

Technological advances, such as satellite communications and e-mail, now make it easy to contact people anywhere in the world at any time. The Internet offers easy access to vast amounts of information that in the past would have taken days, or weeks, to collate; and computer technologies enable us to do more in less time than ever before. Other modern conveniences abound – for example, fast foods, cell phones and air travel. If we can fulfill our responsibilities at home and at work more quickly than before, then theoretically we should have more time to relax and enjoy ourselves. If only life were that simple!

All these benefits of modernity have negative consequences as well as positive. In the computer age it's easy to fall into the trap of spending more and more time at work trying to become ever more

productive. Fast foods have con-
tributed to an increased prevalence
of obesity and diabetes in developed
countries. Ease of travel can result in
our being away from family and
friends more than is good for us.
And being accessible outside working hours to clients or co-workers
via our cell phones can cause work
concerns to invade our home life.

We are more likely than previous
generations to change jobs regularly and to move to different regions
or even different countries. On the one hand, this flexibility gives us a
great chance to meet new people and sample a wide variety of cultural
and working environments. On the other hand, it may make our lives
feel unstable, especially as the growing trend for organizations to hire
people on fixed-term contracts means that often our job changes are
dictated to us.

In identifying the choices that are right for you, the first thing you
need to develop is a clear and compelling vision, so that you always stay
focused on your goals and priorities when scrolling through the often
bewildering range of options available.

The power of vision

As a child, you may have dreamed of doing something great one day. That was the beginning of your "vision". Everyone knows that vision means having the ability to see. When you have a vision for your life, you see a future that you want to make real. If your vision is powerful and compelling enough, it can provide the impetus to turn the future you envisaged into a reality, because every vision, no matter how fantastic it might seem at first, has the potential to become a reality.

The individual who has no guiding vision is like a ship drifting at sea on no set course. On the other hand, the person with strong

vision sees possibilities in their future, which they are determined to realize. The power of vision inspires creativity and resourcefulness and empowers you to reach your full potential.

You can do anything with the rest of your life – what will that be? We are too quick to see things that are beyond our current capabilities as impossible, now and for all time, and so we give up before we've even begun. Yet, if you take a good look around you, you'll probably find someone like you currently doing precisely the thing that you wrote off as unachievable.

Your life vision needs to be bifocal, taking in both your immediate and your distant future. You must focus not only on your ultimate goal, which in some cases may lie many years ahead, but also on the inter- mediate objectives along the way, such as the exams you might need to pass each year to graduate from college.

At a very practical level, your vision serves to organize your goals and priorities within a clear timeframe and sets for you a direction and a destination. It draws on what is most important to you – your values, hopes and dreams. The intermediate goals that you set help you to identify benchmark achievements along the route. In this way, your vision gradually builds, gathering momentum as you move toward your destination, energizing you and motivating you to keep going until you reach your goal.

Think about how your life would look if you identified a master plan and then deployed every available resource and opportunity in order to achieve that purpose. That would be your vision. Such a vision might look something like this: I will be very successful in my career and enjoy it very much; I will live in my ideal home and have everything I need to live comfortably and happily; I will share my life with those I love – my family and friends – and have plenty of time to enjoy leisure activities with them; I will make sure that I get enough exercise, sleep and proper nourishment to maintain my mind, body and spirit in peak shape; I will control my finances so that I can adequately provide for my family's needs; I will make steady progress toward the goals I have set for my life's achievement and legacy.

You can create your vision through a combination of thought and action. Start by identifying the values and principles that guide you in life; next, create objectives to achieve those important things over time; then prioritize to make the best use of your time and be sure that the most important things get accomplished. You will have to manage your time well to be highly successful in your efforts. As you take these steps, your vision will materialize, but it will not be set in stone – you will need to refine it regularly throughout the remainder of this book, and indeed, for the rest of your life, as you continue to seek balanced living.

Dream the possible dream

Your values, hopes and dreams are the wind behind the sails that propel you through life toward the vision you espouse. What possibilities do you see for your future? The creativity, imagination and passion that you had in your childhood are still an integral part of you. Reconnect to them now.

1 Remind yourself of past daydreams you had about your future and note them in a journal (see pp.30–31). Whenever you find yourself dreaming about the future, write your thoughts down.

2 Think about what you might do if there were absolutely nothing holding you back. Write down everything that comes to mind.

3 How do you want people to remember you? What would you include in the "edited highlights" of your life?

4 What elements do you want in your life: marriage? children? fulfilling career? high income? travel? living abroad? Have you left anything out?

5 As your vision starts to take shape, does it excite you? Do you feel eager to get started? Make sure that the vision reflects your own aspirations, not what you think is expected of you. Refine your vision into an adventure in which you can believe and invest wholeheartedly. Map out your route. What's the first step on your journey? Can you take it now?

Racing with time, not against it

There never seems to be enough time to do everything you want to do. Therefore, you should be as adept at budgeting your time as budgeting your money. Look for time economies wherever you can. By spending less time on running and maintaining your home and work, you will have more time available to spend on other areas of your life that might provide more fulfillment and satisfaction, such as your relationships with friends and family.

Learn to prioritize. This includes learning to say no and avoiding committing to things you don't want to do; delegating responsibilities to others; creating strategies for dealing with interruptions; and planning ahead realistically. Resist the temptation to overfill your schedule, so that you don't waste your time trying to rearrange appointments when earlier commitments overrun. Know your own strengths, weaknesses, and those of the people around you, and plan accordingly. Don't forget to schedule some slack time to handle those last-minute surprises and crises, and add some time for replenishing your energy reserves and sharpening your mental faculties. A few minutes of relaxation can dramatically increase your output.

Effectively utilizing available resources – whether you call it asking for a show of friendship, networking, or calling in a favor – is a skill that's frequently overlooked. Some people find this difficult because they don't want to give up control or feel beholden to anyone else, or they think no one else can carry out the task so well. It comes down to choosing to use your time to do the things you do best and enjoy most, and finding other resources to take on the rest. Barter your skills, chores and responsibilities with others who offer something that you lack. For example, an accountant might help a keen gardener with his or her tax return in exchange for some horticultural help.

Another way to economize is to double up some of your routine tasks. Plan your errands to combine several purposes into one trip. For example, think ahead and buy all your greeting cards at the same time, do your grocery shopping for the whole week, call ahead or check on the Internet for prices or availability before making a special trip, and have regular items, such as newspapers, delivered. Motivate yourself to achieve essential but unappealing household chores by combining them with enjoyable activities – for example, you might schedule your ironing to coincide with your favorite radio or TV program.

Setting priorities

Priorities help you to decide how much time to attribute to each of the often conflicting demands you face all the time. Priority-setting is a means of breaking down your vision into sequential, manageable steps that keep you moving in the right direction from day to day.

Accordingly, priorities have to be fluid, because they change over your lifespan as your circumstances alter and your vision evolves. As significant people enter and exit your life (partners, children, friends, relatives), your focus and plans will change. Priorities also change with promotions, job changes and retirement. The day-to-day minutiae of juggling responsibilities, work, home, family, relationships, finances, health and leisure, as well as other people's priorities, can easily side-track you. However, regardless of your life circumstances, clearly set priorities will help to keep you focused on achieving your overall vision through the myriad distractions that go with life.

As you clarify your priorities, specific goals and objectives will naturally begin to take shape as a structure around which to organize your time (see exercise, p.27). It will soon become apparent which goals need to be achieved first. You can then establish benchmarks to track your progress over time. Establishing a program of this kind will help you to manage your time more efficiently.

When setting your priorities consider the following points:

Attend to the most important things first, because you might run out of time if you start with unimportant matters. They may not always be the most appealing tasks, but they will bring you the most benefit.

Prioritize what you do well – don't force yourself *needlessly* into tasks you don't enjoy. Managing your resources well means in part that you focus on what you do best and seek help for the remainder.

Don't value an outcome according to your time or monetary commitment. A highly desirable outcome might occur slowly over time or it might be achieved quickly. Each achievement has an intrinsic value unrelated to any time or monetary resource spent to achieve it.

Becoming a parent is a life-changing event. You'll change some of your priorities, but many do not automatically have to go by the wayside. You'll have to be flexible enough to accommodate your new circumstances into the overall plan. You'll need to reconfigure your time and energy to maintain a proper balance between your child, partner, family, career, finances, and so on. This can be quite a juggling act: although some priorities (for example, travel) will recede, others, such as saving for your children's college education, will come to the fore.

It's easy to give lip service to a priority and then neglect it. Health is a good example. Many good intentions are voiced about exercise and proper diet, only to be relegated to the "when I get around to it" category. Setting a priority establishes a commitment to follow through; otherwise, it's not a priority.

Priorities reflect your values. You will only commit to achieve something that you value. Your values can be anything positive – love, honor, honesty, integrity. Don't be afraid of being old-fashioned or high-minded in picking your values. Your satisfaction and sense of fulfillment in life depend upon the values you choose, and no one else can make the appropriate choices for you.

Remember that you have a duty to yourself. This is easy to forget when we're busy taking care of other people, but we quickly become less useful to anyone else if we neglect our duty to ourselves.

Identify your goals

Identifying your goals isn't necessarily as simple as sitting down with a blank sheet of paper and writing a list. The following exercise is intended to prompt you to name specific goals and also to explore the underlying needs that you hope to satisfy by achieving them. Remember that there's more than one way to meet each of your needs.

I   Gather together a stack of old magazines. Leaf through them, cutting out any images or extracts of text that make an impression on you. At the simplest level, it could be a house that you'd like to live in, or a car you'd like to drive – even a recipe you intend to cook. Look out also for less direct material – perhaps a picture of a person who looks happy with their lot in life or a quotation espousing principles you identify with.

2   As far as possible, sort your cuttings into the following eight categories:

Work, Home, Family, Financial, Personal, Leisure, Social and Spiritual.

3   Stick the cuttings onto a large sheet of card or paper in a circle, keeping them in their categories. Leave space around them for you to write notes exploring why each item appeals to you, what it inspires you to achieve and how you want to feel when you've achieved it. For example, a picture of a marathon runner might inspire you to train for a marathon or it might represent another long, arduous challenge, such as studying for a degree.

How balanced is your life?

You have begun to scrutinize the major areas of emphasis within your life. Since life is full of ups and downs, it's a constant challenge to stay on an even keel. During each day, a multitude of interests compete for your time and attention. What you emphasize in any given moment may result in significant consequences down the road. Therefore, it's essential to know where you are in the process as you continually refine your strategy to achieve the desired balance.

Given that your life is in constant flux, it can be difficult to assess your current state of balance. However, if you don't know where you are now and where you're headed, you'll never know when you've arrived at the destination. Moreover, you'll have little or no idea where to start, what to do, how far to go, how close you are to succeeding, or what the best use of your time would be in any given moment to help you continue to move forward toward your goals. The exercise, opposite, will help you to see how balanced your life is – particularly at the outset of your journey, but also at various staging posts along the way.

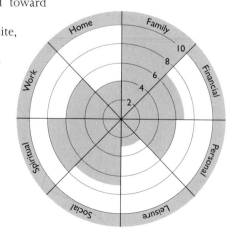

Take your life for a spin

The life-balance wheel (see diagram, opposite) provides an easy way to check your point of balance at any given moment and to plot your progress over time. All you will need to do this exercise is a pen, some paper, a few moments and a reflective mood.

1 Draw your life-balance wheel following the example opposite. It doesn't matter if it's not an exact circle – a rough sketch is fine.

2 Using a scale from 0 to 10, rate how fulfilled you feel in each area of your life (0 = completely unfulfilled; 10 = completely fulfilled). Transpose these scores onto your wheel by drawing lines at the appropriate point along each spoke and shading each of the segments produced. For example, the person who completed the diagram opposite feels 70% fulfilled in the financial aspect of his or her life.

3 Now it's time to assess your wheel. If you feel equally fulfilled in all areas, the wheel will be perfectly round and spin smoothly. But if some areas score much more heavily than others, the ride gets bumpy. Then again, you might find that your scores are similarly low in each area. In this case, the ride may be smooth, but you're not living up to your potential.

4 Your wheel makes it easy to see which areas of your life need the most attention and where you stand in each area. Repeat this exercise any time you want to check your balance. Keep a record each time.

Tracking your progress

Bringing balance to your life is a gradual process, which means that without a record of your progress you may not be aware of just how far you've come and whether you're on the right track. We strongly recommend that you start keeping a journal or workbook, in which you make a note of your objectives and the steps you've taken and plan to take to achieve them (see p.27). You can also use your journal to track your life-balance wheel scores (see pp.28–9).

Get into the habit at the end of each day of recording any occasions during the day when you had to choose between conflicting demands,

and how you resolved these dilemmas. For example, there may be times when you're under pressure to work later than you had intended, jeopardizing a social engagement or a regular gym session. In this way your journal will raise your awareness of issues that repeatedly threaten your equilibrium, which will help you to anticipate them and find ways of overcoming them. It will also draw your attention to any recurring difficulties you are having in meeting your objectives. You may be trying to eat a more healthy diet, but you're lapsing into old, unhealthy eating habits. Perhaps your proposed diet change is too abrupt, making you rebel against it. Should you make the transition more gradual?

Besides being a marker of your progress, your journal will also help to restore your spirit at those times when you're drained of energy and motivation and have lost touch with the vision that you're working toward. At those low moments, you'll be able to go back to your journal to remind yourself what your quest is all about.

Many people are reluctant to keep a journal, thinking that it's a waste of time or that they're not good enough at writing to do it justice. However, the point of keeping a journal is to galvanize you to do the things that will help you achieve your goals, not to win the Pulitzer Prize (unless that's one of your goals). Write down your thoughts without editing, in note form if you prefer. No one but you will ever see your journal and so all that matters is that it makes sense to you.

Career

If you're a working person, your job or career will usually provide one of the key roles in your life. As well as contributing financially, it will influence your self-esteem and your sense of fulfillment. To achieve a balanced life it's crucial to have a clear vision of what you want from your job and to use that as a measure of how well your job is currently meeting your needs.

In this chapter, we'll first look at what you're seeking in your career, how you're performing in it so far and how you might address any dissatisfactions. Then we'll focus on how to use your time and resources as effectively as possible in the workplace situations you're likely to encounter. We'll examine the role of planning, the questions of workload and job satisfaction – and finally how to live effectively and happily with your job outside official working hours.

What do you want from your career?

If you have a job, your career will probably be one of the most important things in your life. It will be vital to your self-image, your sense of yourself within social and family settings, and your level of fulfillment – in short, your happiness. To be healthy and happy, it's essential that your work occupies the place you want it to occupy – or somewhere not too far removed. If, as a result of work, you're making sacrifices now for the sake of benefits in the future, try to have a clear and accurate view of both losses and gains. Unless you feel that the trade-off is operating in your favor, you'll need to redress the balance.

We work not only for money, but to acquire a certain lifestyle, a sense of belonging, of being a part of something meaningful. Ideally, work brings pride in a job well done. But there's no point in denying it, work can also be a burden that often weighs heavily upon us.

Job dissatisfaction can manifest itself as tedium or stress. You might think that you're not on top of your responsibilities, or your workload; that people above, beneath or around you are not pulling their weight; that you're insufficiently appreciated; or that your current job has reached a dead end. Everyone has to face problems such as these at certain times in their life. The trick is to locate sources of stimulation and satisfaction in your job while at the same time finding effective ways to deal with the inevitable stresses and frustrations.

Don't forget that your perception of how much you're enjoying your job and how you're faring in your career may change from one day to another, and is often affected by factors outside the workplace – how well you're getting on with the people closest to you, how well you're sleeping, even what you had to eat last night.

The importance you attach to your job may also vary from one time to another. A career is like a river in limestone country – sometimes highly visible, sometimes disappearing underground for a while; sometimes a raging torrent, sometimes a mere trickle. This applies particularly to parents, who might take a break to stay at home with very young children, but at other times might feel a responsibility to focus on their careers so that they are able to provide well for the family.

Sometimes you might find yourself in a job that doesn't suit you – either the job, or your needs, have changed, leaving you marooned. Or perhaps you've taken a wrong turning somewhere along your career path – not surprising, given that a career usually involves a gamble about the future, and that you face a dilemma at every fork in the road. But whatever the prehistory of your predicament, you stay in this unsatisfactory job, despite the damage to your well-being. While it's not a good idea to quit a job on impulse, you should only stay for as long as it takes you to assess your situation, decide upon an appropriate response, and take the necessary action. And in fact, this process of assessment/response/action constitutes a review that you should per-form routinely, at intervals, whatever your current level of job satisfac-tion. It's a way to focus your attention where it's needed – on your actual situation as compared with the optimum. Are you where you want to be? If not, why not? And why not do something about it?

When you're caught up in the day-to-day issues of a job, it can be hard to take a step a back and review the situation. It helps if you can formulate a set of ideals against which to calibrate the reality. The Career Importance and Satisfaction Questionnaire (opposite) is intended to help you clarify your vision.

CAREER IMPORTANCE AND SATISFACTION QUESTIONNAIRE

This chart will help you to identify the aspects of your career or job that are most important to you and to rate your current level of satisfaction in each of them. You can add any additional concerns if you wish. Give scores out of five for each attribute, first for importance, then for satisfaction, using the two scales below:

Not at all important	Not very important	Quite important	Very important	Extremely important
1	2	3	4	5
Not at all satisfied	Not very satisfied	Quite satisfied	Very satisfied	Extremely satisfied

	How important?	How satisfied?
1. Salary		
2. Working conditions: hours, responsibilities, work policies		
3. Job security/stability		
4. Support given by managers/executives		
5. Professional development		
6. Opportunities for advancement		
7. Job title/position/prestige		
8. Compensation package		
9. Manageability of workload		
10. Opportunity to use my talents and knowledge		
11. Compatible with my values		
12. Intrinsically interesting		
13. Altruistic: benefits to other people		
14. Enjoying the work I do		
15. Enjoying the people I work with		
16. Scope for my creativity		
17. Allowance for flexibility and change		
18. Personally challenging		

Career change or makeover?

Everyday frustrations in your job may push you toward change just for its own sake. However, such an automatic response will not usually provide the best solution – or even a good solution – in the long run. Be as strong and purposeful as you can. Think of yourself not as needing to get away, but as needing to be in a better place, the *right* place, within a certain time-frame. Don't just wildly press the button of the ejector seat: instead, firmly take the controls, set a sensible course, and look for somewhere suitable to land.

On the other hand, people often resist making a move, even a move that would be right for them, because change is scary. The seductions

of the "comfort zone" are familiar. Anyone who decides on change faces the challenge of an unknown future: not only a new job, but also new people, a new environment, a new culture. Maybe it's easier to stick with the devil you know. You might even find yourself inventing pretexts for staying – for example, ascribing too much importance to peripheral benefits, such as free company products, proximity to good shopping, or colleagues you couldn't bear to lose – in order to convince yourself or others.

In plainer terms, if you feel dissatisfied in your job, you must decide whether to stay or to leave; and if you opt to leave, you must decide what moves might make sense for you, how to choose between the different options available to you, and how to put your choice into effect.

To help you appraise where you stand, examine your ratings in the Career Importance and Satisfaction Questionnaire (see p.37). Note which career aspects you rated as most important and then look at your satisfaction scores. If these ratings are low, then those aspects of your work that matter most to you are not living up to your expectations, and you'll probably want to consider making some changes. On the other hand, if the ratings are high, you might decide that no changes are necessary; or you might decide to look at other aspects of the job that are of less importance to you, and tweak them.

Often it will take analytical thought, plus imagination, to come up with solutions. For example, your analysis might tell you that your salary expectations are satisfied, but you're spending too many hours at work and don't have enough time for the rest of your life. In such situations there's no magic wand. You'll often take a series of measures, each of which will contribute to the desired result. You might set yourself a deadline for leaving the office each day, give more thought to sharing your workload, say no to extra responsibilities that you don't have time to take on ... and so on. Or you might decide to make a more dramatic change, such as renegotiating your working hours.

It's very common, when faced with work dissatisfaction, for people to perceive themselves as having limited options; and, indeed, sometimes there *are* limitations, such as the fact that only a few employers within your field operate in your local area. Moreover, when you've been in a job for a long time, you tend to forget that you have marketable skills. Without a true sense of your own worth, you're unlikely to make the right move. So explore the opportunities, and don't dismiss any for which you're well qualified on paper just because you believe that in practice you'd be out of your depth.

On the other hand, don't decide too hastily that a job change is the answer. If you look for things to be unhappy about in your present work, you'll find them. Conduct a thought-experiment, making small imaginary adjustments to working methods, processes, reporting lines, resources and workplace environment; see if some of the apparent disadvantages disappear. Consider also whether third-party pressure, from peers or family, is pushing you forward against the grain of your intuitive wisdom. It isn't immoral or immature not to be ambitious.

You might decide that your job is basically fine but could stand a little fine-tuning. If so, make this the subject of a special meeting with your boss. Be clear what you want and ask for it plainly. Propose solutions based on opportunities you identify, rather than simply stating problems. You want to be seen to solve problems, not cause them.

A complete career change, if you need one, can take place at any stage of your working life. The old tendency to value youth against age is losing ground. Focus on the many marketable skills that your experience offers. Network to find out what opportunities are available to you. Start to train for a new job before you leave your old one – especially important if your finances won't allow any break in your income.

Becoming self-employed or working from home will often be tempting. It offers greater autonomy and more flexible working hours, and it may facilitate childcare. The potential drawbacks include reduced financial security, loss of company pension and healthcare benefits, loss of the social dimension, and the blurring of a psychologically useful division between work and home.

Planning your work day

All too often we spend our working days putting out fires, only getting to our priority tasks at the end of the afternoon. Although you can never eliminate the unexpected, there are ways in which you can protect yourself from its corrosive effects on your time.

Start your day by setting aside a little time to decide what you intend to accomplish that day and how long you'll need to spend on each task. Prioritize the tasks that absolutely have to be done that day, so that if you run out of time the things left on your list can wait until tomorrow. At the end of each day, review your progress.

If you consistently underestimate how long it takes you to achieve work tasks, try keeping a time log for, say, a month. List each job, note how long you think it will take and then note how long it actually does take. This should help you to become more accurate in your estimations and thus avoid overstretching yourself.

External distractions, particularly if they arrive by phone or in person, can be hard to ignore. The person standing

Take the work out of paperwork

Paperwork (including e-mails) is an inevitable aspect of our working lives. Trawling through endless memos and forms can be tiring, but not as tiring ultimately as watching them pile up and worrying about not having dealt with them. By assessing each item using the following system, you can reduce the energy drain that paperwork creates.

1   Whenever you receive a document or e-mail, quickly classify it using the 3-D rule: Do it, Dump it or Delegate it. The aim is to handle each item no more than once, so that it doesn't accumulate into unmanageable piles.

2   "Do" the task associated with the paperwork if you've got time; "Dump" it in the recycle bin (or delete it from your computer) if it's unimportant or you can access the information elsewhere; or "Delegate" it if there's a more suitable person than you to handle it.

3   There is a fourth D – Defer it – which you should only resort to under certain circumstances. Be careful not to abuse it. It's justifiable to put to one side a piece of paperwork that you can see is going to require more mental effort than you can call upon at that time. However, you should reschedule it for a time of the day when you are typically at your most alert. Don't defer the same task more than once.

4   Using this method on a regular basis will reduce the time you spend dealing with and worrying about paperwork.

in front of you will demand your attention more urgently than any-thing on your desk. One solution to combat such distractions is to mark off an hour or so of your day in which you switch your phone to voice-mail, log out of your e-mail and ask your co-workers not to disturb you, except in case of emergency. You may find this discipline difficult at first, but after you've experienced the benefit of accomplishing your key tasks in a focused way, you'll soon find that it comes much easier.

Internal distractions, such as daydreaming, focusing on tasks other than the one in hand and self-criticism, can also get in your way. That internal dialogue can be a powerful force keeping you from doing your work. It might tell you, "You need more information," or "It won't work anyway, so why bother?" You must recognize that your alter ego who thinks this way is a saboteur. Listen to the contrary voice, then refute it. "I can proceed for now without that information." "It has worked before, so why shouldn't it this time?" Try also taking a mental vacation (see exercise, opposite). This will help you to interrupt your negative inner voice and return ready to refocus on your work.

No matter how diligently you plan your workday, nasty surprises still arise. However, they don't have to derail your plans entirely. When a real emergency bites, take a while to reschedule your priority tasks not yet addressed for that day. Delegate. If you make it clear that this is an emergency, people will rise to the challenge of a heroic rescue.

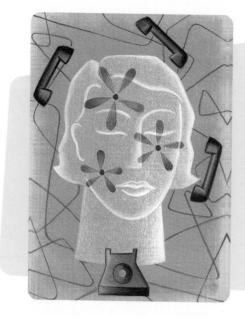

Go on a mini mental vacation

Vacations are intended to give you a break from your regular routine and return you refreshed and energized to focus on the tasks at hand. This exercise shows how you can experience these benefits without leaving your desk. When you are struggling with a task, allow yourself a brief mental "vacation" to re-energize you, rather than grimly persevering only to become more and more frustrated, tired and demoralized.

1 Close your eyes and focus on your breathing. Breathe in slowly and deeply through your nose, then breathe out slowly through your mouth. Your body will automatically relax in response to this type of slow, deep breathing.

2 While you're breathing deeply, imagine a soothing scene. For example: relaxing on a beach with the sound of crashing waves; camping under the stars; sitting by a mountain stream; hang-gliding on a warm, sunny day; sitting in a cozy chair in front of a fire; or lying in a bubble bath surrounded by aromatic candles.

3 Spend several minutes on this mini vacation, experiencing it with all of your senses. Enjoy how relaxed you feel.

4 When you're ready to return to work, remember where you are before opening your eyes. This will ease the transition. Tell yourself that you'll take with you the feelings of relaxation and energy that you gained on your mini vacation.

When to say yes, when to say no

In the average workplace, each person has a defined job function. However, it's not always clear who is responsible for every duty that may arise, which means that you'll often be asked to take on additional tasks. And when a co-worker is particularly busy, you may step in to relieve the pressure on them, as you'd expect them to do for you.

This collective sense of responsibility is essential to every successful organization. However, there may be times when your willingness to help out leaves you overburdened. You may think that refusing to help is rude, or selfish, or even taboo. However, to be most useful to your employer, you have to recognize which tasks are your priorities and ensure that you have enough time to do them. If you overcommit yourself, you'll leave people thinking that their task is in safe hands, only to let them down later – too late. Or you'll work longer and longer hours in an effort to keep up (see pp.48–9). Neither approach is good for your career, for your health or for anyone else.

Keeping these considerations in mind, you should be able to turn down an impossible request without causing offence. Don't be embarrassed to say "no"– saying "maybe" when actually you mean "no" is misleading. Explain why you're not able to spare any time on this occasion, but offer any advice you can.

Identify your drainers

There are many aspects of work that can sap our energy without our realizing it – unsolicited phone calls, red tape, a cluttered desk, irritating background noise, and so on. This exercise expands on the "time log" concept (see p.42) to help you become aware of these insidious energy thieves. It's only by identifying our "drainers" that we can find ways to counter or eliminate them, and so boost our energy levels.

I   In addition to keeping a record in your time log of how long it takes you to complete each task you undertake, make a note of all the things that interrupt you and how long each interruption lasts.

2   Be aware of occasions when you feel anxious or annoyed or distracted. Enter the time into your log and the most likely explanation for your mood.

3   Analyze your time log after you've been keeping it for a week or so. Which interruptions occur most often? How much time do you lose to interruptions or distractions each day? At what times of the day do they most commonly arise?

4   Starting with the worst culprits, think of ways to deal with your energy drainers. For example, if you're regularly distracted early in the afternoon, make this a time to do tasks that require relatively little concentration. Or if you waste time looking for things on your desk, get into the habit of tidying it at the end of each day.

Time to go home

How many hours per week do you work? Overtime can become a way of life, but it takes its toll. If you find your working day keeps over-running, ask yourself: Why am I working so many extra hours? Is my workload unreasonable? Have I overcommitted myself?

Working hard can be hugely rewarding in terms of both satisfaction and salary. However, if your working day monopolizes your time to such an extent that you neglect your family, social activities and spiritual or intellectual pursuits, then your work may be costing you more than you're gaining. You should step back, examine your reasons for working long hours and come up with counter-arguments. For example, if you perceive it to be necessary to work overtime in order to keep up with other employees, remind yourself that what counts is not the number of hours you spend at work but what you achieve while you're there. Working overtime may actually undermine your performance. Commit to going home by a certain time, no matter what. Commit to leaving work at the workplace and living your life fully at home.

The same applies if you work from home, only you must be even more diligent about separating your home and work lives, because the two become so intertwined. A close-of-business ritual might help, such as changing clothes or taking a walk or doing some other exercise.

Make a virtue of commuting

An important, but often underused, period of our working day is the time we spend traveling to and from work. These transition times can help you prepare for the next phase of your day — by either planning the work ahead or unwinding ready for home.

On the way to work

1 Make a reminder list of home-related concerns and how to tackle them, so they don't preoccupy you at work.

2 Prepare for your day. Set your priorities (taking notes if you're not driving). List the things you need to do to accomplish these priorities.

3 Review your schedule to make sure it will allow you time to achieve your objectives. Modify it if necessary.

4 If you're feeling nervous about an upcoming challenge, remind yourself of your past successes to help you tackle the task with a positive attitude.

On the way home

1 Use your journey home like a diver's decompression chamber. Review what you've achieved at work, plan for the next day, then file away your thoughts about work until tomorrow.

2 Shift your focus to home or your personal goals. Consider how you're going to spend the evening, plan dinner, or simply use the time to relax.

3 Depending on your mode of transport, you might listen to an audio book, a language course or music, practice singing, read, plan your vacation, write to a friend, and so on.

Money

There seems to be something almost magical about money. It takes on a power and life, even perhaps a will, of its own. In an increasingly commercialized world, it's easy to lose perspective when dealing with money – to revere it and to see the acquisition of wealth as a goal in its own right.

However, money is nothing more than a resource to give you choices about how you live your life. The better you manage your money, the more options you'll have available. In this chapter, we'll examine the role money plays in helping you to achieve your goals and implement your plans for the short term as well as for the medium and long term. We'll learn about the financial management tools that allow you to control money to serve your needs – for example, how to save imaginatively and to invest and borrow sensibly.

What does money mean to you?

At the simplest level, money is merely a medium for transactions. Yet many people find money management intimidating. It may seem too technical for them – or perhaps just plain boring. People who think of money as frightening, magical, mysterious or tiresome often surrender control of their finances to someone else; or, worse still, they make no provision at all for money management. While it's wise to consider the financial advice of experienced people, never forget that the ultimate responsibility for your finances lies with yourself. Always have a stake in decisions relating to your financial well-being. The way

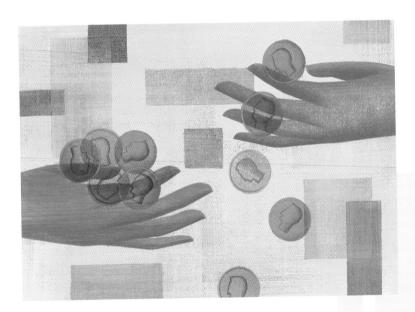

you handle money, like your treatment of your home, your car or your clothes, reflects your values. Potentially, money has an important place in anyone's value system.

Money is a key to freedom. However, in a balanced life it's only an enabler, not a goal in itself. To make money work for you, you should aim to strike the right balance between spending money for present necessities and enjoyment, and saving and investing for future security. There is also, of course, a role for giving – even if you have only a little to spare, this can be richly rewarding.

Like time, money is a finite resource that you should deploy in line with your priorities. You can't "have it all" in material terms – something usually has to give. It's easier to manage your financial resources well when you clarify what's most important to you (see pp.24–7). For example, if spending as much time as possible with your children is a priority, then you might decide to reduce your working hours. In order to make up for the resulting drop in income, you may have to spend less on lower-priority areas, such as vacations or new things for your home. You need to *make* choices in order to *have* choices.

Always think of the value as well as the cost of your expenditures. For example, if you spend a certain amount on eating out with a friend you haven't seen for a long time and you come home with warm memories of an enjoyable evening and a friendship renewed, then that expense gives you more value than spending the same amount going out for a meal simply because you haven't got the energy to plan, buy and cook a meal at home.

Look out for your weak spots. What tempts you into "low-value" spending? It might be new clothes or CDs, or something less easy to quantify. Perhaps you are "comfort spending" – the financial equivalent of eating a donut. Such spending is frequently an attempt to lift our mood, although the improvement is usually short-lived. What other, less expensive ways might you find to give yourself good feelings? For example, consider taking time to listen properly to music, go for relaxing walks, visit museums or galleries, or try out new recipes. You could still go shopping but limit your spending by taking a designated amount of cash with you and leaving your credit and debit cards at home.

Using money well is good for the spirit. When we host a party, we create an abundance of good will and emotional satisfaction. Using money badly is bad for the spirit. Think how you feel when you owe serious money to a friend or let credit card debts get out of hand. Using money well is often an extension of using time well. Short-term pleasures are usually gained only at the expense of the long term. But at the same time, if we invest only in our future, we may wake up one day to find poverty in our past.

Where does your money go?

How often do you look in your purse or wallet and wonder why there's so little cash left in there? Money just drains away. By keeping track of all your purchases, you'll gain a greater understanding of your spending habits and you'll be able to see just how quickly the small, apparently inconsequential purchases mount up.

1 Every time you spend any money in cash or by credit card, no matter how little, keep the receipt. Carry a notebook, and record in it any purchases for which you don't receive a receipt. Keep all your records together. If you're living with a partner, ask him or her to do the same.

2 At the same time each week, sort all your purchases into categories, such as Groceries, Going out, Clothes, and so on. Add up how much you've spent in each category and enter the totals into a ledger, or use financial software if you prefer.

3 Looking through your week's spending, can you see any amounts that surprise you? For example, did you realize how much you were spending at the café near work? Make a list of your weak spots and set yourself targets for reducing your spending in each of them.

4 Repeat this exercise each week as part of your "financial hour" (see p.57). Disregard any exceptional amounts, such as your annual home insurance premium, but pay particular attention to the target areas you identified at step 3.

Maintaining your financial health

To manage your cash flow effectively, you have to keep track of your spending (see exercise, p.55). It's best to do this each week, so that you're able to rein in any over-spending before it gets out of hand.

As well as monitoring your weekly outgoings, it makes sense to carry out a monthly analysis. This longer timescale allows you to draw meaningful conclusions and develop a realistic spending plan. First differentiate between essential and discretionary spending. Essential spending (such as mortgage and loan repayments and utility bills) is fixed and non-negotiable. Saving is also non-negotiable (see pp.58–9). Set monthly spending limits for non-essential categories, such as entertainment, dining out and clothes. However, don't make your spending plan unrealistically strict – this will only encourage rebellion.

Regulate your cash flow, to avoid being tripped up by any large amounts that you hadn't budgeted for. For example, open special savings accounts for vacation, Christmas and taxes; and make regular monthly deposits. You'll earn a small interest bonus that way, as well. Whenever possible, set up automatic bill-pay (direct debit) for regular bills, such as your mortgage or utilities payments.

YOUR FINANCIAL YEAR

Managing your finances is easier when done on a regular basis. The following check-list of weekly, monthly, quarterly and annual tasks gives you the framework for your financial year. All of this may sound daunting; but when you actually do it, you'll be sur-prised how quick and easy it can be. Set a regular time each week – your "financial hour". Put some music on. And do something fun afterwards as a reward.

Weekly tasks:

- Gather receipts in one place and add them up
- Note on a bill calendar when recently received bills need to be paid
- Write all checks for payments due during the coming week and ready them for mailing
- File rebates or warranties, and any receipts you might need to return items
- File all other receipts in a discard folder to be thrown away or shredded at the end of the month

Monthly tasks:

- Adjust discretionary spending to account for spending overruns and any unbudgeted new expenses
- Identify and eliminate any "low-value" spending (see pp.53–4)
- Make deposits (e.g. savings, investments, special funds)
- Monitor investments – look out for the best deals on the market

Quarterly tasks:

- Fill in your quarterly tax return, if necessary

- Check how your spending plan is going and fine-tune if required so everything balances by year's-end

Annual tasks:

- Revisit your current spending plan and adjust for the next year if necessary
- Revise your savings plan to accommodate any changes in your goals or circumstances
- Complete your tax return and any other annual financial requirements

Make your money work as hard as you do

To the uninitiated, finance may seem a dry, impenetrable subject. But the more you explore it, the more you'll realize that money is really a whole world of fascinating relationships – cash, debt, inflation, interest rates, property values, investment and liquidity. And besides, knowing how to handle your money wisely is essential for your well-being.

People make all kinds of excuses for not saving and investing for their future. But if you don't, no one else will. No matter how much or how little you earn, discipline yourself to set aside a portion of your

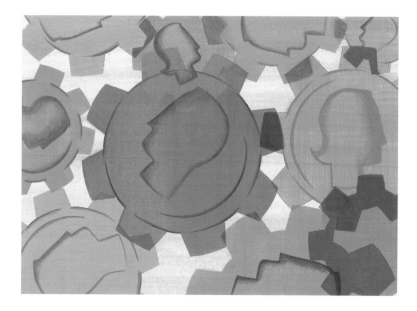

income each month for saving – set up a direct deposit so that it happens automatically. Saving should be factored into your spending plan,
just like your electricity bill: it shouldn't be something you do only if
you have money left over at the end of the month. You won't have. Save
proactively – monitor changing interest rates and move your funds if
necessary. Leaving your savings in an under-performing account
is like letting a slow puncture go untended.

Consider how important it is for you to be able to get
your hands on your savings quickly. If you're saving for a down-
payment on a car or a house, you'll need easy access to your funds. But
when saving for retirement, you can trade off ease of access for the sake
of a higher yield. Consider also how comfortable you are with risk. The
stock market offers higher potential rewards than savings accounts, but
at a risk. As a general rule, you can afford to have a more risky (and
potentially more rewarding) pension plan when you're younger, as you
have time to recoup losses before retirement. However, as you approach
retirement age you should switch to a more conservative strategy – to
protect what you have. Remember the golden rule: never gamble with
what you can't afford to lose.

The more you delve into the economics of your life, the more
fascination you'll find there. Banish the mystique of money: be canny
with cash.

Pain-free saving

Saving at least a little each month is crucial to safeguarding your future. We all fret about interest rates, and we may try various money-management strategies to ensure that we'll gain the maximum yield from our deposits. But real prudence operates by a further strategy: that is, to make sure that the maximum residue of your income is left over from your spending, so that you have more to invest in saving.

To motivate yourself to save, it helps to have a clear idea of what you're saving for. Concerned about the international crisis faced by pension funds in the early 21st century, you might be keen to cushion yourself for a comfortable retirement. But a more acute priority, for the moment, might be to fund the upbringing or education of your children, or a down-payment on a house. There will be times in life too when logistics require you to invest in a new car, or your doctor or stress counsellor is urging you to take a vacation. Also, in a separate account, it's wise to build up an emergency fund equivalent to at least three months' salary to see you through lean times in the event of losing your job or being unable to work owing to injury or illness – this is particularly important if you're self-employed.

You may be wondering how you can possibly find any spare cash to put away when everything you earn is already earmarked for other purposes. If this is the case, you would certainly benefit from analyzing your spending (see p.55). It's easier to find ways to save when you are skilled in the art of spending. The aim is not to deprive yourself of things that currently bring you happiness, but to save money by identifying and eliminating spending on things you wouldn't miss. For example, do you subscribe to a newspaper or magazine that you rarely have time to read? Do you take taxis when it would be relatively easy to use public transport or walk? Do you go to restaurants out of habit rather than as a treat?

Not only might you consider eating out less often, but there are also pain-free ways of reducing your grocery bill. Avoid buying processed food, such as microwave meals. Preparing meals from scratch is cheaper, healthier, more satisfying – and it doesn't have to take much longer. Look for bulk-buy offers – particularly on non-perishable items. You can use similar strategies in each category of your spending plan. For example, high heating bills might be lowered by turning down your thermostat, adding insulation, and weather-stripping windows and doors.

However, try not to feel trapped in constant survival mode. Look for ways to make saving fun. Allow yourself small rewards if you meet your saving targets.

Responsible borrowing

We are often warned of the perils of borrowing money. However, there's no reason why debt shouldn't form part of a balanced life. Borrowing enables us to achieve significant goals, such as owning a house, going to college or starting a business, that might otherwise be out of our reach. When there are items or experiences that would profoundly enhance your life satisfaction, that fit with your vision and priorities, and that you will never be able to afford unless you borrow money, then responsible borrowing may be the route to choose.

Unfortunately, it's all too easy to lose control of our borrowing, so that instead of ourselves managing our debt, it manages us. A common mistake is to borrow right up to the limit of what we can afford to repay. This is fine while circumstances stay as they are. But life is constant change. We may lose our job, or start a family, or interest rates may rise. What had been a manageable debt now becomes a huge, destabilizing burden. The following watchpoints are to help you guard against borrowing pitfalls, or to cope if you're faced with a debt problem.

Repaying your debt must be your financial priority – even ahead of saving, because a borrowing interest rate is always likely to be higher than a savings interest rate. That's how banks make their money. The sooner you can pay off a loan, the less it will cost you.

Be careful about borrowing from family or friends. There are obvious attractions – for example, they may not charge much or any interest, and they're less likely to take you to court if you default. However, borrowing money from people you know can place a significant strain on the relationship. If you do go down this route, put the terms of the arrangement in writing to avoid misunderstandings.

Don't borrow on your credit card. A credit card is a convenience, especially when paying over the phone, on the Internet or when you're abroad, but it's a very expensive way to borrow, and it's easy to lose control of credit card debt. Monitor your transactions each week – ideally, don't put more on your card than you can afford to pay off in full each month. Your credit limit is a ceiling not a target.

Be honest with your creditors. If you've fallen behind in repaying a debt, don't hide from the problem. Creditors are more sympathetic toward people who talk to them rather than ignoring their reminders. Negotiate with them – they want to see their money again, so it's not in their interest for you to implode financially. Agree a repayment plan that you can keep up with until you get back on your feet.

Treat yourself

We've been talking so far about being responsible with your money – by managing your finances wisely, economizing, saving and reducing debt. However, it's possible to take this too far, so that guilt stops you from spending any money on yourself. Money is a resource to get you the things you need. And one of your needs, surely, is to enjoy life.

Is there an item or event that you'd really like to purchase for yourself (or your family), but have been putting off? Why are you putting it off? If you think that you don't deserve it, why do you feel this way? How much harder would you have to work or how much more money would you have to possess before you could justify treating yourself? The chances are that your "worthiness threshold" will always remain tantalizingly out of reach, in which case now is as good a time as any to commit to your enjoyment.

Maybe you really do intend to purchase this item, but currently you can't afford it. This is a budgeting issue. If you decide how much you can set aside each week for, say, your vacation, or your new car, then you'll be able to calculate the date on which you'll reach your target. Seeing your savings gradually build up week by week will heighten your enjoyment of your treat when you've finally saved enough to pay for it. And you'll certainly feel that you deserve it!

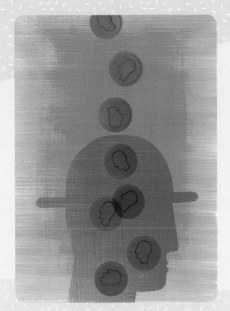

Exercise 9

Invest in yourself

Investing in your personal development is the wisest investment you can make, and the payback will last a lifetime. Studies have shown that people who regularly participate in some intellectual, artistic, social or spiritual pursuit tend to live longer and in better health than those who do not. The following exercise will help you to decide how you want to invest in yourself and how to convert intention into action.

1 Make a list of ways in which you might like to invest in yourself. Some may be relatively simple, such as seeing a play. Others may take more planning – such as studying for a degree.

2 For each item on your list, write down how much time and money, and what materials and information, you'll need to make this happen.

3 For those projects that will require an extended time commitment or a large financial investment, devise a preliminary schedule to help you budget and focus on one stage at a time.

4 Put one of your plans into action this week. If you have limited time, choose something relatively simple. Otherwise, you might start a bigger project.

5 Schedule some "self-investment" time into your calendar at least once a month – although once a week would be better, as your "dividends" would be greater.

Relationships

Relationships are woven into the fabric of life. In one way or another, almost everything we do involves contact with other people. Many of your contacts are likely to be with casual acquaintances – people you meet every day, from the mailman to the local storekeeper, but whom you never really get to know. Then there are the close friends you accumulate at each stage of life. At any of these stages you may meet someone who becomes your life partner. And then, of course, there's your family, some of which has been with you from the start.

In this chapter, we look at how all relation-ships contribute to the balance of a life, and we explore how you can make your partnerships, friendships and family bonds as fulfilling as possible, in themselves and in relation to your life's overall pattern.

Relationships and the individual

Most people are sociable by nature and tend to gravitate toward each other. Meaningful and satisfying relationships provide all manner of benefits, such as intellectual stimulation, experience to learn from, humor, emotional or financial support, encouragement, responsiveness, inspiration, and a sense of belonging, acceptance or security.

Being in a relationship of any kind requires that you take into account the needs of the other person – their interests, priorities, responsibilities, schedule, and so on. Failing to attend to balancing the needs of both people contributes to disappointment and dissatisfaction.

Relationships are living savings accounts. If you expect them to remain in the black, then you have to keep investing in them; otherwise the debits will reduce the balance until there's nothing left. Many relationships fall short of their full potential as a result of lack of attention and maintenance. Set aside some time to attend to your relationships and work at keeping them healthy.

Sometimes different relationships will conflict with each other – for example, your partner or spouse might not like one of your friends or relatives, or vice versa. In such circumstances, you might be inclined to smooth the situation over by complying with the desires of one or other party. But often you'll find yourself conducting a juggling trick, applying fine judgments to what you say or do, and giving due attention to ensuring that both your relationships stay on course.

Many individuals seek a special partnership to satisfy their needs for companionship, sex, family connections, children, and so on. And most societies promote marriage as an ideal. However, some people find that their needs are better served by remaining single. What would be lonely for one person is liberating – or at least comfortable – for another. A glance at recent demographic trends in the US and UK shows that a greater than ever proportion of adults has never married, and that the marriage rate has been steadily decreasing over the past 30 years.

It's accepted wisdom that if you're living life to the fullest, enjoying your interests, enjoying being who you are, then opportunities to find a like-minded partner will come your way. However, it's not always so simple. Many find themselves still searching after many years. Search too persistently, too single-mindedly, and you might find yourself neglecting other aspects of life. Desperation, even in its milder forms, either puts people off or leads to unsuitable choices.

If you're single and would prefer not to be, it helps to know what you're looking for – which personality traits, habits (vegetarian or non-smoker?), opinions, interests. A tolerant temperament goes a long way toward creating an auspicious relationship – even more than shared interests. However, even a tolerant person might find certain habits and views (especially political and moral) hard to take.

Some people advocate that reluctant singletons should make a concerted effort to "market" themselves. Certainly, it makes sense to think about how to present yourself in terms of manner and appearance, and where to advertise yourself for maximum exposure. Certain leisure activities lend themselves especially well to meeting new people – for example, tennis clubs, reading groups, various gym-oriented fitness groups, political clubs, and so on. Blind dates, set up by well-meaning friends, can be surprisingly fruitful – though it's wise never to have exaggerated expectations.

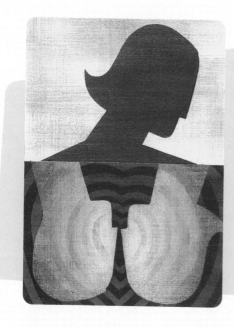

Relationships
inside-out

Take a closer look at your relationships to see how they stack up in meeting your needs. Relationships play a range of different roles – some are core, others supplementary. Go through this questionnaire to check that you have a workable balance.

1 Refer back to your list of priorities and goals from Chapter 1. Map out which of your current relationships relate to which priorities and goals. For example, if being creative is important to you, which of your relationships reflect this priority?

2 If some relationships don't really fit any of your priorities or values or drain your energy, do they otherwise hold value for you? Perhaps they bring lightheartedness or just plain enjoyment?

3 Do you have priorities or goals that none of your relationships satisfies? If so,

can you enhance any of your relationships to meet those needs?

4 Do you have enough relationships of differing depths to fully meet all of your requirements?

5 Do you have more than one relationship that you can really count on in difficult times? Beware: relying too heavily on one relationship can put a strain on it.

6 Do you enjoy most of your relationships? If not, what would you change about them to enjoy them more?

The balanced partnership

To keep your relationship healthy, you'll need to spend some quality time alone with your partner. Otherwise, eventually, the intimacy, passion and commitment you feel for each other may dwindle. Couples who have the most satisfying long-term bonds usually continue some of the practices of their dating years to keep the relationship fresh. Going out together is still seen as a date. No matter how busy and chaotic your lives become, you should make such dates a priority – whether at home or out and about. Share thoughts and feelings on a daily basis. Go for walks together. Dine out together whenever you can, in a spirit of romantic luxury – this is easily worth the cost of a first-rate meal plus a babysitter's fees.

Healthy partnerships also have to strike a balance between togetherness and the independence of the individual. Spending too much time with one person, no matter how well you get on together, can become stifling in a way that starts to weaken the relationship. It's likely that you will have some interests not shared by your soulmate, and you should be able to express any unique talents you have without feeling bad that he or she won't be able to share them with you. Some couples even find it desirable to spend some vacation time apart – whether visiting relatives separately or enjoying a leisure interest with friends.

Over time, even with the best intentions, we may end up taking our partner for granted. In our busy lives we may allow other commitments to commandeer the time we previously spent as a couple. This can happen insidiously, without our realizing it. It's one of the downsides of feeling comfortable with each other – you imagine that you no longer have to work at the relationship as a project. In this word "project" lurks an important cue. Whatever the pressures (for example, the disorienting impact of retirement or the unsettling emptiness of the nest after the fledglings have flown), you'll be better equipped to deal with them if you continue to work at your relationship as a life project, instead of treating it as part of the furniture. Be watchful, read the signs, redress the wrongs, analyze and learn from the mistakes.

Weighing up the big decisions

Making big decisions – to commit to someone, to live together, to start a family, to separate – is a challenge most of us have to face at least several times within a lifetime. Sometimes we have to tussle with a dilemma alone, sometimes it's a shared problem. It's always good to have someone else to help flesh out the issues and to brainstorm with – even if they're not involved in the situation, they may be able to come up with perspectives you would never have encountered unaided.

All big choices have a practical dimension, but reason alone is probably not going to lead you to the right decision. Most dilemmas have an emotional component as well. The best decisions will probably be based on a blend of the rational, the pragmatic and the emotional.

When two people are faced with a big dilemma, one might want to plunge in, the other take things more cautiously. Although this might cause tension, such a mixture of dynamism and circumspection often brings a happy resolution in the long run. While respecting the other's needs and feelings, you must be willing to express your own. Don't worry if some of what you hear makes you feel uncomfortable – an implicit aspect of decision-making is the working through of differences, some of which may have prevented you from coming to this crossroads sooner. Anger is the worst reaction: it's unacceptable to be

angry merely because someone is telling you how they feel.

Inertia – the drift factor – prevents many decisions from ever being made. If you find yourself shying away from an important decision, find a way to motivate your-self to action. One extreme would be to book yourself into a hotel room and not leave until the decision is made and clearly written down – but there will usually be other ways of simulating this kind of pressure, even in your own home. Alternatively, see if you can sample the expe-rience in question, or something like it. If you're not sure whether you want to try to have children, spend time with a friend who has chil-dren – perhaps even go on vacation with them. Try visualizing yourself in the changed situation you are contemplating and seeing how it feels. Do this with your partner perhaps, building up a detailed word-picture like a pair of storytellers. Visualizing a successful outcome will help you commit to taking action. Beware of self-deception – of reasons that are really just pretexts ("Let's live together, it will be cheaper"; or "Let's spend the vacations apart to recharge our relationship").

Having made your decision, be faithful to it. Declare a no-fly zone for regrets. If problems arise, tackle them. Don't look back.

Sharing in partnership

When you pool your talents, knowledge and experience with those of another person, you're able to do so much more than you could ever have done alone. However, juggling a balance of temperaments, wills and impulses within a relationship can be tricky. People like to be in control, and that often creates a strain. Individuals have to find ways to cope with sharing control of their space, their time and their energies with another person. It's not easy; but when it works well, the rewards are outstanding. Under modern-day pressures, the support and reassurance of another person can make all the difference. Not to mention, of course, the shared enjoyment, the camaraderie.

To make any relationship work, each partner must clearly understand his or her own role and responsibilities within the arrangement as a whole. Otherwise, resentments fester and productivity suffers. When each person contributes fairly to doing the requisite tasks, there's more time to enjoy each other and life generally. If one person is so busy that they

never have time to break out of the endless cycle of chores, the relationship will suffer until eventually someone will discover that it isn't there any more. Loving, attentive sharing keeps the balloon aloft.

Within the typical work environment there are schedules, reminder notes, assignments, deadlines, contracts, and all kinds of structures to make sure that expectations are communicated and objectives are accomplished. Similar strategies can work at home, too. House meetings are a good way to clarify who is responsible for which chores, to establish timelines, and so on. Such meetings also promote an appropriate mutual respect and understanding. Other helpful techniques include a family bulletin board to post reminder notes and a calendar of activities. Cell phones and answering machines make it easy to provide reminder calls and to leave messages of encouragement. Develop a system that works for your household.

A common obstacle to effective cooperation is disagreeing over how or when things should be done: how or when to wash dishes, or deal with the neighbors, or handle the laundry. Which jobs are pressing and which can wait? Then there are the countless issues surrounding finances, parenting, healthcare, and so on. When we've been used to doing something a certain way, it's easy to forget that there are other, equally valid approaches. Never browbeat your partner. The spirit of the happy home is democratic. Tyrannies usually end in a revolt.

Balancing work and childcare

In the past, raising children was simpler: one parent stayed home while the other worked. Today, that is no longer the norm, and it can be quite a challenge to juggle the demands of work with those of parenting.

As a woman returning to work after maternity leave, you'd probably find it distressing to leave your child in childcare. You may feel selfish for partly opting out of parental routines, and then when you're at work you may feel equally selfish for not giving top priority to your job any more. Many women describe a double disappointment: in their failure at work and as a mother. Be honest with yourself and your employer about what you can and can't achieve at work. And don't judge yourself against either full-time, stay-at-home parents or full-time, childless co-workers. "Superwomen" are mythical beings.

For a childless person, work is often the most stressful element of their life. However, a parent may actually consider their job to be light relief from the round-the-clock responsibilities of having a child. Guiltily enjoying their working day, parents may try to compensate for perceived neglect by overspending on gifts and treats for their children (perhaps adding to the financial burden). The chief wage earner may feel compelled to earn more for the children's sake, while the other feels guilty for their lesser contribution. Some working mothers make only enough to cover childcare costs. The reason for going back to work is not necessarily to earn money, but to have a more rounded life.

To find a work–childcare balance that suits your circumstances, you'll need to be flexible, creative and realistic. For example, if the mother is the higher wage earner, it might make sense for the father to stay at home as househusband – although it can be hard for a man to relinquish the provider role that society traditionally expects of him. Yet another option is for one or both parents to work at home, thereby enabling more flexibility to achieve an equitable division of responsibility. Although small children need full-time supervision when awake, it may be possible to schedule work for times when they are asleep; alternatively, when your partner comes home from work, he or she may still have the energy to take over childcare for a while.

There's a saying that it takes a whole village to raise one child. However, changes in social structure, such as families moving apart geographically, have made it harder for the extended family to take over the village's role. Some couples move closer to their parents to rectify the problem. Others form new communities – particularly with other parents they meet at pre-natal classes. These groups are well qualified to provide emotional support, as well as practical help in the form of reciprocal childcare arrangements, which have the added benefit of helping children to develop socially through contact with their peers.

Fulfilling friendships

Friends can help you balance your life in all kinds of ways. Different friends fulfill different needs: some might provide entertainment, others might offer you such gifts as insight, encouragement or sympathy. If you're single, friends will be your social lifeblood. If not, they can help you gain fresh perspectives you wouldn't otherwise acquire.

Many people feel more free to talk about certain matters with friends than with family. Within most families there are taboo subjects – uncomfortable areas to be avoided so as not to cause concern or upset. That's not to say that friends may not also have taboo subjects. It's just that you can be more open in setting ground rules with friends, because the topics in question tend to be less sensitive than those within families. For example, work friends might make it a rule not to discuss work after hours. Other friends might agree to limit the time they spend talking about subjects such as their children or vacations.

Friendships are elective – that is, voluntary. We choose them, and it's beneficial to make wise choices. Friends can also become habitual. Old friends have a special place in our affections – especially when they are our only contact with a certain phase of our lives. However, if you find that you only talk about the past with such a friend, the value of the friendship may fade. Even the best of friendships can be neglected and fizzle out over time. Usually this results from life changes, such as having children, changing jobs, moving house (see box, below), retiring, or just becoming so busy that you lose touch with each other.

Intuitively we believe that we shouldn't be too calculating about our friendships – to decide, for example, to drop a friend seems heartless. But there may well be times when it would be totally justifiable to do just that. For example, a friend might betray your trust, their values

TRIUMPHING OVER DISTANCE

Maintaining a friendship can take a considerable effort, especially if the friend in question lives far away. Often communications become less and less frequent, until they become mere updates rather than intimate discourses. On the other hand, distance can sometimes enhance a friendship. For example, you might find that on those rare occasions when you are in the same place as your friend, you make it a priority to see them. Ironically, you may even see them more often than friends who live near by – perhaps you take it for granted that you can see your local friends anytime you wish, and so you seldom make the effort to do so. Some friends actually become closer with distance: the fact that they are prepared to invest the extra effort to keep in touch makes them realize how much they mean to each other. With e-mail, written communication can be almost instantaneous – more like a telephone conversation than an exchange of letters. E-mail friendships acquire their own special flavor, and can sustain deep intimacy – rather like the sharing of a diary. Always avoid saying anything in an e-mail that you'd be mortified for your friend's partner or offspring to see.

might diverge from yours irreconcilably, or they might expect more from the friendship than they are prepared to offer themselves. Whether you just let such a friendship fade away or take direct steps to sever the connection depends on the seriousness of the breach and on how comfortable you are with conflict.

It is, of course, more positive to cultivate new friends. It's good to have friends from different walks of life, for their different perspectives. Friends have the potential to exchange skills – so get yours to teach you their specialisms. They can offer an "open sesame" to new experiences. Yet many parents may feel somewhat trapped in a social circle limited to other couples who are parents (see p.79). If your friendships are narrow in scope, ask yourself if that's by choice or by circumstance. If the latter, you might choose to seek out further opportunities for friendships that are probably available with a little extra effort, or see if you can broaden the horizons of the friends you already have.

We tend to think in terms of having a finite group of friends. When we want to go to, say, a movie, we'll ask a friend along. If none of our close friends seems interested, we may give up on the idea. However, some people would have no inhibitions about inviting someone they hardly know – and why should they? Initiatives of this kind break through social straitjackets and can lead to valuable new friendships.

Stay in touch

Most friendships need regular attention to remain healthy. However, it can be hard to find time to do them justice, with the result that, without meaning to, we let good friends drift away. Take the following steps to clear time for your friends.

1   The next time you or a friend says, "We should get together sometime," whip out your diary and set a date. Don't just let it go: "sometime" never comes.

2   Pick up the phone. If you're not sure how to start the conversation, try "I was just thinking about you."

3   E-mail is an easy and quick way to let someone know you are thinking of them or to make plans. For a more special approach, hand-write a quick note or card. You can even do it for someone you see all the time – they'll appreciate it.

4   Plan regular get-togethers. For example, you might choose to host a monthly brunch – nothing fancy, just a reason to meet and catch up on a regular basis. Better still, consolidate a network of friends by taking turns hosting.

5   Introduce new people to your circle from time to time – for example, you might occasionally bring someone from work, or from your yoga class, to one of the brunches (see point 4). This avoids the pitfall of only seeing your friends in a particular social setting, which may lead to a sense of staleness.

Family matters

The family has been subjected in modern times to various disruptive pressures. More marriages end in divorce, meaning that more children grow up with just one parent. More young adults leave their home region to seek work elsewhere, so that families become scattered. Despite these changes, our families continue to give us valuable support, encouragement and a sense of belonging. Often, though, it's only when our family ties unravel or when we face adversity that we realize just how important our family is to us.

CELEBRATIONS

Family celebrations have developed a bad press. The image of bickering relatives trapped together over the festive period is a staple of soap operas and sitcoms. But in real life, most family gatherings are much happier affairs. Tensions tend to relax, if there are any; or, if they do come to the surface, there will usually be someone who knows how to soothe ruffled temperaments. If you're hosting a family celebration, with food and drink, consider the following points:

- Don't make things too complicated, or you're likely to get stressed. Plan your dishes and shopping in advance. If you don't actively enjoy cooking, choose failsafe dishes, with some of the food prepared in advance. Delegate work to others in the family.
- Always keep the purpose of the celebration at the front of your mind. Invest love and joy in all stages of the occasion. Enjoy the break from routine, even when you're doing chores like washing the dishes. Enjoy the symbolism of the family get-together.

We each decide what value to place on family ties, although usually there's an unstated hierarchy. Most people have no difficulty identifying their obligation to their parents or children, but at the outer limits of the network, responsibilities tend to blur – a cousin may mean less to you than a friend. There's no need to feel guilty about this. However, part of the value of family is the fund of shared memories, and as the older generation passes many people find that links with relatives provide a living memorial.

Even the closest family relationships may become strained. Childhood rivalry between siblings may persist into adulthood; teenagers asserting their independence may alienate themselves from their parents. However, whereas neglected or abused friendships might die away, family ties are more resilient. In a crisis, families often set aside their differences and provide each other with the unconditional support we may be reluctant or embarrassed to ask for from friends.

This is why we tend to take family for granted. To prevent this, make a point of celebrating birthdays, anniversaries and public holidays with them (see box, opposite). Keep in touch. Alarm bells should ring if you haven't spoken to your parents or children for, say, a week. Be there for them even when they're being difficult: this phase will pass.

Giving something back

People have different reasons for giving their time and talents to the community in some way. Having received many benefits, we may decide that it's time to give something back. We may be looking for a way to do something that extends our social network, uses or develops our talents, offers an outlet for our charitable impulses, or helps to make positive changes through local politics. Regardless of our motives, such investment of time and energy is likely to be rewarding – provided that it reflects our values and makes us feel that we're genuinely making a difference, however small.

As we've seen, each of the ways in which we spend our time contributes to the overall balance of our lives. Contributing to the community can help this process of balancing by providing a counterweight within the inner mechanism that constitutes our self-image. For example, charitable work may help to weigh against a feeling that we're excessively privileged, perhaps through our parentage, social class or education.

In the way that lawyers often do *pro bono* work, for no fee, we might donate our professional skills to the community: an electrician might do the lighting for a local drama group, or a printer might work on community bulletins and flyers in his or her own time, without charge.

Having made a commitment to become involved, it can be daunting to take the first step. We're not all natural leaders or "joiners". To help you in the early stages, you might ask whether any of your friends are interested in accompanying you. Your first port of call might be one of the various organizations of which you're already a passive member – perhaps a church or your children's school. There are also websites that put volunteers in touch with all manner of charitable foundations. You might soon find yourself helping children with their reading, clearing waste ground for a public garden, or pitching in at a local crisis shelter or drop-in unit. The possibilities are endless. Even if you have only one or two hours a week to spare, and even if those hours have to be spent at home (for example, for childcare reasons), there'll be something you can do to help, and you'll be richly blessed in return.

Home

Apart from the workplace, most people spend the greatest proportion of their waking time at home. Common sense tells us, therefore, that it should be a comfortable place to spend time, and not just somewhere to eat, sleep and store your possessions.

Whether you own or rent, a home is more than your greatest financial investment: more importantly, it's a personal project, an extension of some of your values. The approach you take to this project will greatly influence the quality of your life.

This chapter will help you explore how to create a home environment in balance with your personal needs. We'll see how your home can inspire and relax you and your family, as well as give you pleasure. And we'll look at some of the many dilemmas you'll face with regard to choosing or changing your home.

Move or adapt?

Once you've analyzed what attributes are most important to you, you can decide whether to move house or to adapt your existing home.

People who choose to move sometimes make costly mistakes, and the dream home can turn into a nightmare. When this happens, they rapidly fall out of love. Ask yourself a question: "I've fallen in love with this house – but am I prepared to marry it?"

Don't feel that you're necessarily being foolish or self-indulgent if emotional factors loom large in your choice of a home. But be aware of precisely what the emotional value is, and what you'll sacrifice. You might be interested in moving to a larger house or a better location,

while wondering if this is really going to be the wisest option. Consider whether you foresee changes in other areas of your life, such as your finances, job and family, as these may have an impact on your decision. Moving house can disrupt the balance of your life or redress that balance: don't move at all if you feel that the balance won't be tilted toward the positive.

If you decide to stay where you are, consider what you can do to make your home as comfortable and suitable for your needs as possible. You might build an extension, update your kitchen, bathroom or décor, or redesign your garden – perhaps to incorporate an eating or play area. Be ambitious and creative in your thinking. You can add space without calling in the builders simply by making an existing area serve an additional function that hadn't occurred to you before. For example, the space under the stairs might accommodate a work desk, which can be stowed away unobtrusively when not in use.

Some people will be happy simply to live in a relaxing, pleasant environment, but others may want to focus their budget on a specific piece of equipment that will bring them and their families a great deal of enjoyment. It can be very rewarding to customize your own space so that personal or shared family interests can be pursued to the full (for example, by installing a state-of-the-art music system or making a family room double as a home cinema for special "movie nights").

Some people become uncomfortable with their surroundings if they don't redecorate at least every five years, whereas other people genuinely prefer a more "lived-in" look. If you're irritated by chipped or discolored paintwork or wallpaper that's outstayed its welcome, then redecorating will almost certainly help to improve your relationship with your home. Some themes can be less expensive to bring to life than others – rustic charm tends to cost less than metropolitan chic. Washable fabrics might be worth considering, especially if there are small children around.

Remember to give due attention not only to the appearance but also to the routine structural maintenance of your home. Pre-empt problems before they even arise – for example, it's a good idea to get your boiler serviced each year, rather than have to call out an engineer when it breaks down during a cold snap. Similarly, repaint exterior woodwork every five years or so, to save yourself the worry and expense of dealing with rotten window frames.

Depending upon your abilities, you might be able to do some of the work yourself. This can save a lot of money and be fulfilling. However, be realistic about what you can and can't achieve (particularly when tackling electrical work, plumbing or heavy building). It can end up costing more to bring in professionals to correct your mistakes than if you had hired them to do the job in the first place.

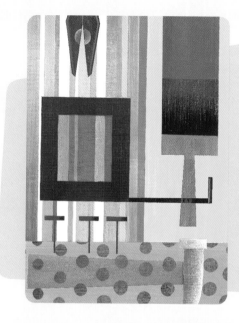

Look through
the keyhole

It may not seem a particularly significant thing to do, but adding light personal touches to your home can help you feel more at one with your surroundings. What's more, a little effort can go a surprisingly long way. Here's a procedure for assessing how well each room of your home reflects your personality and correcting any imbalances.

1 Choose a room in your home, preferably one in which you spend a lot of time. Stand in the doorway and look into the room. Try to imagine that you've never seen it before. What impression does the room give you? What features strike you most immediately? What sort of people would live in a room like this?

2 Ask yourself to what extent the room speaks of your personality. Does your individuality come over too strongly? If so, you might choose to remove some of the personal touches.

3 On the other hand, you might decide that the room lacks the stamp of its owner or owners. If so, you might choose to personalize it more. You could add some art that's especially to your taste or change the predominant colors to make a bolder statement.

4 If you still feel that the room doesn't reflect your personality enough, look for some unusual object – a sculpture or a modern antique. Eastern objects are now imported inexpensively, and would make a good starting-point for your quest.

Creating a haven

A haven is a safe, welcoming place to retreat to when we need a break from the energy-sapping hurly-burly of everyday life. Typically, we associate the word "haven" with tranquillity, stillness, contemplation. You'll probably want your home to provide these qualities, particularly if they're lacking from other areas of your life. However, there's no set formula for creating a haven. Some people find Zen-like simplicity relaxing – just a few well-chosen objects on show, and a deliberate avoidance of visible clutter. Others, however, find serenity in a rustic ambience, cocooned amid hand-crafted earthenware and antique farm implements.

We all need to recharge our batteries in the home, and to do this we need to be able to draw energy from our surroundings, rather than let dissatisfaction with our surroundings draw energy from us. So the first golden rule is to make sure that in the rooms where you choose to relax, there are no nagging reminders of jobs crying out to be tackled. The ideal haven wards off thoughts of domestic chores as well as professional ones.

Think about the things that give you the most pleasure, and if possible make sure that your home supplies them. Perhaps you love the invigorating effect of a powerful shower: if so, invest in the best shower system that you can afford. If you like hiding yourself away in your bedroom, buy beautiful, sensual bed linens.

Fresh flowers add a touch of natural luxury to any room, and are always worth the expense. Choose long-lasting flowers if you're on a tight budget – maybe start off with sprays of ferns or foliage from the garden, or from a neighbor's. To maximize the benefits of favorite things, look for ways to combine them. For example, if you enjoy listening to music and spending a long time soaking in the bath, you might consider installing a sound system in your bathroom.

Lighting is the key to mood in most homes, and you should opt for maximum flexibility – lots of low-level lamps to provide localized lighting at night, when it's comforting to sit in distinct pools of light.

If you have a garden or backyard, it may exist in two different dimensions – as a place to sit, relax and garden; and as a view through one or more of your windows. It's worth concentrating any expenditure in the garden on the view you see from inside, as the mind readily fools itself into believing that what isn't visible doesn't really exist (which, incidentally, is why we banish our clutter to cupboards rather than disposing of it). If all you have is a small backyard, a climbing plant up a trellis and a small ornamental tree in a pot will probably be enough to create the required mood of contemplative relaxation.

Apartment-dwellers often derive pleasure from cultivating indoor plants (which also improve air quality) or tending window boxes overflowing with masses of spring or summer flowers or herbs for cooking. It's as if the natural instinct to stay in touch with nature were satisfied by even a small symbolic garden. A similar symbolism operates in landscape paintings and zoological or botanical prints, all of which create the illusion of opening up a claustrophobic room.

If you work at home, your workspace should inspire activity and be free from the distractions of home life. However, at the end of your working day, you need to be able to shut your job away. This is possi-ble even if you don't have a separate office – ideally, buy a workstation that folds up into a cabinet, or certainly make sure that you put away every last piece of paperwork and computer kit relating to your job. Similarly, if your living room doubles as a play area, encourage your children to tidy away their toys before they go to bed.

A well-organized kitchen can contribute enormously to a stress-free home life. Make sure that the utensils and ingredients you need to use most frequently are stored in the places that are easiest to access.

Conduct a comfort audit

You may have noticed that you feel particularly comfortable in certain areas of your home. There may be other areas that you don't really like to spend time in. Use this exercise to assess what makes you feel more at ease in some rooms than in others.

1 First, consider questions relating to the whole of your home, such as: Which rooms are most functional and which do you seldom use? Which areas do you use for specific activities (such as reading or paperwork)? Which areas are most relaxing and which most unwelcoming?

2 Walk from room to room and observe the things about each room that please you and the things that trouble you. Make a note of your observations.

3 In each room, ask yourself whether the furniture is placed to facilitate good traffic flow and seems to belong in the space. Is the room either too crowded or too bare? Look out for gloomy areas that need more light and areas that are too bright and harsh. Consider whether the pictures and decorations enhance or detract from the room's appearance.

4 Think of ways to duplicate some aspects of the "best" rooms in the less comfortable ones. And ask yourself how you can make better use of neglected areas. For example, if you rarely use your dining room, you might decide to have a special family meal in there each Sunday.

Clutter-busting

Most people accumulate more possessions than they need or know what to do with. We may have an atavistic survival instinct that makes us reluctant to throw away anything that may one day prove useful to us. Yet most of us find clutter stressful: it impinges on our equilibrium, like a migraine. The balanced life has few superfluous possessions.

Clutter builds up little by little, so the best way to keep on top of it is to deal with the situation regularly. The basic principles are very simple: throw out all trash and put in its rightful place everything you've finished with. Establish a filing system for paperwork. Set aside 15 minutes each day to straighten up your living spaces. Wash dishes immediately after eating, even if there are only a few pieces. Periodically clear out anything you don't use anymore and donate it to charity or sell it.

If your clutter problem has crept out of control, more radical action may be required. We often form attachments to possessions, perhaps because they remind us of happy times or people we love. This can make it upsetting to throw certain things away. However, it's impracticable to turn everything we've ever owned into a souvenir. Launch yourself into a major clear-out, enlisting the help of family or friends. As well as providing muscle power, they'll be able to offer objective advice on what you can keep and what you really should get rid of.

The 15-minute daily tidy-up

One habit that will serve you well is to spend 15 minutes every day tackling the areas of the home where clutter accumulates. A quarter of an hour may not seem long, but by making it a deadline, you can achieve an amazing amount.

1   Choose one area that needs your attention: for example, the pile of unsorted mail, the kitchen drawer, or the dusty knick-knack shelf.

2   Set a timer for 15 minutes and begin tidying up. Don't stop until the 15 minutes have elapsed.

3   Sort items into separate piles according to where they should end up: for example, "storage", "donation", "trash", "proper location for use", or "rearranged in current location". Just throwing things in a drawer to hide them only transfers the problem. Take the opportunity to dust or clean any surfaces you have cleared.

4   When your timer rings, assess your progress. Congratulate yourself on what you've achieved. If you think you need to spend another 15 minutes, go ahead, but don't overwhelm yourself.

5   Repeat this every day for at least a week to begin to establish the habit. The longer you keep it up, the easier and more effective it will become over time. You'll be surprised at what you can accomplish in sessions of just 15 minutes.

The balanced weekend

For anyone who works from Monday to Friday, weekends seem to take forever to arrive. Then from Friday night, time flies and before you know where you are it's Monday morning again. If you try to pack in all the things that you haven't had time to do during the week, there's a danger of those precious two days bursting at the seams. You'll probably want to see friends or relatives. If you have

DO YOU REALLY HAVE TO WORK THIS WEEKEND?

Are you constantly bringing work home with you or going into the office at the weekend? In most jobs, there are times when working at the weekend is hard to avoid, but if this becomes the rule rather than the exception you may need to make some changes.

When we're under pressure at work, we often lose our sense of perspective. We may feel compelled to work at the weekend, but end up achieving relatively little, because we're tired from the outset. If you're contemplating doing some work this weekend, ask yourself some questions to help you decide whether it's a good idea.

• When was the last time you worked at the weekend?

• Do you feel that you're making this decision on your own terms, or do you feel that you've no choice but to work at the weekend?

• Have you been feeling particularly tired or stressed lately?

• Will doing this work relax you more than it tires you?

• What would happen if you left the work until Monday?

children, you'll also want to spend some quality time with them (especially if they're usually asleep by the time you get home from work during the week), as well as with your partner. You may have leisure interests to pursue. Then there are regular chores, such as cleaning, laundry and ironing, and perhaps some home maintenance projects. However, if your weekend becomes ruled by never-ending to-do lists, you may find yourself going to work on Monday morning more tired than you were on Friday evening, and so your break won't have carried out its function of refreshing you for the week ahead.

Schedule into your weekend at least one or two periods of slower time, giving you 10 to 15 per cent more time than you think you'll actually need. If you finish the activity sooner, so much the better: you'll have time for a coffee or a chat. If you're rushing somewhere immediately after an early breakfast, make sure that you get some relaxation time later in the day – perhaps idly reading your paper after lunch instead of in the morning.

Mark the weekend out as special and do things that are a little unusual. For example, you could take the opportunity to explore some of the areas of your neighborhood that you don't know well. Many of us have tourist or leisure sites on our doorsteps that we assume are of more interest to visitors than to locals – but why should this be so? If you have the time, you could even make part of the weekend a mini-vacation, spending a whole day away from home somewhere not more than a couple of hours' drive away.

Weekends offer a useful way to extend vacations, because five days off work becomes a nine-day break. However, you might enjoy having a seven-day trip followed by a leisurely home weekend more than tailoring your trip to fit all nine days available: your time off work will probably seem longer that way, and you won't have to deal with such a dramatic culture shock on the Monday morning you resume your working life. Instead of taking a two-week vacation, it's worth considering having one week off, followed by a week at work, followed by a further vacation week, as this gives you two vacations of nine days, making 18 days, rather than 16. It also makes the return to work less stressful, as you can catch up during the middle week.

Weekends are for chores and for parenting, as well as for adult leisure activities. Efficiently attending to tasks will give you a satisfying sense of jobs well done and make you feel that you deserve any idle time or treats afterwards – which perhaps is a good reason for scheduling the tasks for Saturday mornings. To be efficient, prepare for your chores during the working week by doing any necessary shopping in advance. A big shopping expedition is a feature of many people's weekends, but with a little ingenuity (including use of the Internet) you can avoid this.

Saturday night is a prime time for giving a dinner party, and many hosts find that they spend the whole day preparing: devising the menu, tidying up, shopping and cooking. With a little forethought some of these tasks can be done in advance, leaving you with more energy to enjoy the party. Many choose to be ambitious with their cooking, not because they enjoy it, but because they believe that they have to make a special effort for friends. That's

fine, but make sure that you don't overstretch yourself and compromise your own enjoyment of the evening.

No matter how well you balance your weekend, there may be times when you suffer from "Sunday evening syndrome" – characterized by anxieties about the week ahead and difficulty getting to sleep. Often we go to bed on Sundays earlier than on Fridays and Saturdays, but it can be tricky to reset our body clock to working time. On Sunday evening your priority should be to unwind. Do something gently enjoyable. Don't go to bed until you feel tired: prepare yourself for sleep by following a pre-bedtime routine (see p.129).

Health

Many people think that good health is something that only the lucky are blessed with, but this is largely untrue. Unless you were born with a serious illness or condition, you can have good, even excellent health by looking after yourself well. Taking control of your health is a powerful way to influence, not only how *long* you live, but also how *well* you live.

In this chapter we explore how you can achieve well-being through managing crucial aspects of your health. We discover the importance of being pro-active in taking measures to protect ourselves from falling ill; we consider ways in which we can combat stress; and we look at how our diet, exercise and sleep can all be improved. By working on these aspects of your lifestyle, you can enhance well-being both in the short term and the long.

Preventive maintenance

Think of your body as a very complex machine. It has many intercon-nected parts. It runs nonstop for years. In order to work properly, it needs to be filled with the appropriate fuel. It has mysterious inner workings that only specialists understand; and it can break down if it's not properly maintained. If you want to keep in top shape, it's wise to carry out preventive maintenance and take action at the first sign of any problem. You can prevent malfunctioning by monitoring your body and doing periodic checks so that you can diagnose any impending problems and fix them before they become serious.

SEEING THE DOCTOR OR THE DENTIST

Even the most health-conscious person needs to see a doctor or a dentist occasionally. However, many people put off seeing a health-care professional until their problem becomes unbearable. By that time, the options for successful treatment may be more limited than if they had seen someone earlier. Some people erroneously believe that "what they don't know won't hurt them," or they claim, "I can't afford treatment," or "I don't have the time." In this way they allow their fears to put their health at risk.

You should always see your doctor or dentist when anything causes you concern – for example, if you're in great pain or if you think that your symptoms are lingering longer than they would if you had only a transitory condition. If you're not sure whether you need treatment, monitor your symptoms and make a point of going to see your doctor if they worsen or you feel more ill.

When you see your doctor be ready to describe or show them what's wrong. Explain when the symptoms appeared, how severe they are, and whether they've worsened or improved. This information will help your doctor to make the correct diagnosis. He or she will probably examine you and then prescribe treatment.

Monitoring your health isn't difficult, but it does require a little time and effort. Start by making an honest assessment of your current state. Ask yourself questions such as Do I feel well? Do I eat nutritious foods? Do I take an adequate amount of exercise? Do I get enough sleep? The answers to these questions will give you an overall picture of your well-being and will also highlight any areas you need to improve. (We explore the topics of healthy diet, exercise and sleep in greater depth later in the chapter.) Then, record your assessment in your personal health record (see exercise, opposite), for future reference.

Next, find out about your immediate family's health. This will help you to discover whether you're at risk from a hereditary disease, condition or allergy. If there's a health problem in the family, make sure that you acquaint yourself with the first symptoms so that you can seek medical attention immediately if they appear. Again, note down anything important in your health record.

Another useful form of preventive maintenance is to visit your doctor once a year for a check-up. Regular medical check-ups are necessary to catch cancers, heart disease and many other conditions that are curable in the early stages. Visiting your dentist every six months and your optician once a year are also important components in a preventive maintenance program.

However, be careful not to become obsessive about your health and rush for treatment before you know that there's anything wrong. Although it's hard to say when vigilance becomes obsession, if you consistently see symptoms that turn out to be false alarms or you're making yourself ill with worry, your concern about your health may be out of balance. If this is the case, see your doctor to reassure yourself that you're not sick. Then consider seeking professional help for your anxiety if you find that you're continuing to worry.

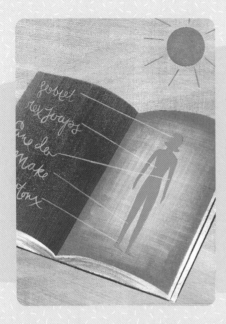

Keep a personal health record

A good way to take charge of your health is to keep a written record of your personal medical details. Note the following information and keep it in a safe place.

1 On the first page, list basic information, such as the names, addresses and telephone numbers of your doctor, dentist, optician and other healthcare professionals, such as your osteopath.

2 Next, write a brief personal medical history. Include the dates of all your immunizations, any major illnesses, surgery and hospitalizations you've had, and any allergies you have.

3 Jot down your assessment of your current state of health, and mention any diseases, conditions or allergies that run in your family.

4 List any medications that you take regularly, whether prescription drugs, herbal remedies, vitamins or dietary supplements, or over-the-counter drugs. (Keep a copy of this list in your wallet or handbag in case of emergency; include any drugs to which you are allergic.)

5 Document your wishes regarding extraordinary life-saving measures and organ donation in the event of your becoming seriously ill or injured.

6 Make sure that your partner or a close family member or friend knows where to find this record should the need arise.

Stress-proofing

Stress is an unavoidable fact of modern life. Even when things are going well, the many, often conflicting demands that we face in our hectic lifestyles can have an adverse affect on our concentration, stamina and many other aspects of our health. However, there are actions that we can take to reduce the negative effects stress can have our well-being and life balance.

We experience stress when we have to cope with issues that we feel are beyond our resources. Major life changes, such as marriage, divorce or the death of a loved one, are stressful because we feel overwhelmed by them and we're unable to gauge whether we'll be able to deal with them effectively. However, the most frequently cited cause of stress is having too much to do in too little time.

The symptoms of stress we exhibit vary from person to person, but some common early warning signs include: anxiety, loss of concentration, irritability, bursting into tears, fatigue and frequent minor illnesses. Often, stress manifests itself in the same way, time and again. Some people always break out in a skin rash just before an important social occasion; others always get a cold immediately after working toward a vital deadline. These physical symptoms appear each time because stress has compromised the body's immune system.

When we feel stressed, we often engage in unhealthy behavior. For example, we might eat comfort foods, or we might turn to alcohol. During anxious times many people sleep poorly, smoke more, give up exercise, allow irritations to damage relationships, perform less effectively at work ... and so on. While we often have no control over the cause of stress (stressor) that occurs, we do have control over our own behavior and how we respond to the situation. Behaving in unhealthy ways may make us feel better at times when we're under pressure, but in doing so we're sacrificing long-term balance and health for the sake of momentary comfort.

To help to maintain balance in your life, you must identify and deal with the greatest stressors. You can take measures to stress-proof your life. Such steps will help you to avoid the negative effects of stress and mitigate them when they do occur.

The first step is to identify common stressors and to analyze what makes them stressful. To help you pinpoint your stressors, ask yourself the following questions: What events or situations do I find difficult? What events or situations do I try to avoid? What daily hassles

seem to sap my energy or drag me down? Once you've identified several stressors, analyze *why* they are stressful for you. For example, perhaps you feel stressed in situations over which you have little control.

Once you've identified and analyzed your stressors, the next step is to plan a course of action to help you eliminate them. This is particularly true if you've tended to avoid certain stressors in the past, but realize that it's now time to deal with them. Exercise whatever control you can muster. Use time management or communication skills. Learn to slow your breathing to calm yourself (see exercise, opposite). Meditate – a practice worth learning if you've never tried it. Or attempt to engineer shifts of mental perspective: for example, reason with yourself that worry isn't going to solve your problem, and that all you can do is respond to *what* happens *when* it happens. Alternatively, look at the situation from a positive angle and view it as a challenge instead of a burden. Or you could discuss the situation with a sympathetic listener if it helps to talk, or if you think they might be able to assist or advise.

Sometimes past experience may offer a way forward. For example, if, the last time your workload increased dramatically, you asked for and received help, the appropriate response is obvious: ask again.

Finally, take care of yourself. If you are well-rested, eating healthily, exercising and have good moral support, you'll be in a strong position to deal with any stress that comes your way.

Emergency stress relief

When we're stressed we tend to take short, shallow breaths, which make us feel worse. This exercise shows you how to use deep breathing to calm yourself down when you're faced with a stressful situation.

I   If possible, sit somewhere peaceful and comfortable. Otherwise, find a quiet corner somewhere. Place one hand on your upper chest and one hand on your belly. Notice which hand moves as you breathe. If you're stressed, the hand on your chest will probably move more, and you'll be taking shallow breaths, rather than using your full lung capacity.

2   Now inhale deeply through your nose taking the air right down into your lungs. Hold it there for a moment, and then gently exhale. Continue breathing deeply like this, filling your lungs each time.

Deep breathing automatically makes your body relax, gives you a rich supply of energizing oxygen, and calms your mind.

3   To enhance the relaxing effect, as you exhale mentally assert an affirmation to yourself, such as "I am calm," or "I am doing fine," or something similar. Or imagine that you are drawing in fresh energy with each in-breath.

4   Practice deep breathing as often as you can so that you'll be able to use it to calm yourself whenever you find yourself in a stressful situation.

Eating well on the go

Healthy food is the fuel our bodies require in order to function at peak performance. When we supply the body with nutritious food and drink, we not only have fewer health problems, but we also feel better, have more stamina and live longer.

As people are on the go so much these days and food is readily available day and night, seven days a week, the choices we face can be overwhelming. It's often tempting to choose convenience foods, such as take-outs or TV dinners, rather than take a little extra time and make a little extra effort to have a healthier meal.

With our busy lives today, it can be difficult to maintain a healthy, nutritious diet. We are inundated with advertisements for junk foods, which are high in fat and calories. Fast-food restaurants abound in almost every neighborhood. Convenience foods take up huge amounts of shelf space at the grocery store. Even prepared meals that you can just pop in the microwave have chemical additives, sugars, fats and more calories than many people realize. Simply finding the time and energy to shop for and prepare healthy food can be a challenge. While it does take time to make meals from scratch, with a little foresight you can have delicious, nourishing meals that take up precious little time in the kitchen.

A little planning goes a long way. If the reason you don't prepare healthy foods is that you never seem to have the proper ingredients, plan ahead and stock up your refrigerator and cupboards. You can buy foods you use often in bulk and either freeze or store them until you need them. This can save you money if you buy your favorite items when they are on special offer, and also save you time because you always have all you need to hand.

Go food shopping once a week so that you can buy everything you need for the week ahead and won't need to pop out all the time for missing ingredients. Take a shopping list with you to ensure that you don't forget anything and to limit impulse buying. Be sure that you visit

the produce section of your grocery store first. If your basket is full of fresh fruit and vegetables, you'll have less room for junk foods.

There are simple steps that you can take to make preparing healthy meals easier to fit into your schedule. Plan your meals for a full week and ensure that you've included enough fruit and vegetables to meet

MOOD-EATING

What do you feel like eating? This exercise will help you make good decisions about eating more healthily. Go through the following quick steps before you grab that snack.

• Ask yourself whether you're really hungry. If the answer is yes, then proceed to the next step. If no, then do something else to satisfy whatever need the snack would have served. If bored, then find something to do. If lonely or bored with your own company, then talk to someone. If you were reacting purely out of habit, then establish a healthier habit to replace this one.

• Ask, What am I hungry for? Do I want something salty or sweet? What kind of texture am I craving – smooth, crunchy, chewy? How hungry am I? By answering these questions, you'll be able to choose a food that satisfies your desires in a quantity that will satisfy the hunger. For example, if you decide that you're hungry for something sweet, smooth and cold, you might choose a yogurt fruit smoothie rather than a bowl of ice cream.

the recommended five servings a day that help to protect your body's immunity. Five servings may sound like a lot, but a serving is smaller than most people think: an apple or a glass of fresh fruit juice, for example. Have some fruit with breakfast, salad with lunch, two vegetables with dinner, and a fruit or vegetable snack during the day.

When you cook your favorite dishes, double the amount you usually make. Use half right away and freeze the other half to use later in the week. Or, divide the food into single servings that you or members of your family can have when you can't eat together. Most casseroles, soups and stews lend themselves easily to this method and include ingredients from several food groups to provide good nutrition. Consider cooking several meals at the weekend to use in the workdays ahead. Your overall time spent cooking will be reduced because you're doing it all at one go rather than spreading it out over the week.

As well as good meals, you'll sometimes need to eat snacks. If you choose the right snacks, they can be an important source of nutrition and help to maintain your energy levels throughout the day. Choose healthy snacks that provide you with a variety of flavors and textures. Try dried fruit when you crave something chewy and sweet; yogurt for something smooth and sweet; nuts and crackers or pretzels for something crunchy. If you stock up on a variety of healthy snacks, you can substitute one of these when you crave candy or chocolate.

The benefits of exercise

There's no getting away from the fact that exercise is good for you. Studies indicate that regular physical activity helps to prevent illness and alleviate pain, as well as supporting the heart, increasing lung capacity, and decreasing the build-up of hormones that cause stress, such as cortisol. Physical activity strengthens the muscles, builds stronger bones and helps to prevent painful conditions such as osteoporosis. Exercise improves flexibility, which in turn helps prevent accidents and injury caused by restricted mobility. It actually decreases fatigue by increasing endurance, improving your sleep and lowering your stress levels.

Exercise also has subtle but significant effects on your emotional state and outlook on life. By sticking with an exercise program, your self-esteem, self-confidence and sense of self-mastery increase as you attain the goals that you set for yourself. Your body image improves as you look and feel better. In short, regular, appropriate exercise is one of the most powerful tools you have available to you in your quest for balance.

Unfortunately, even though we're aware of the benefits, many of us find it hard to get started on an exercise program. As with developing all good habits, taking the first step is by far the most difficult part. We may make all manner of excuses (see exercise, p.123), but actually there's no reason why anyone, whatever their current level of fitness or the amount of time at their disposal, should not engage in some form of regular physical activity. Take things gently at first with simple activities, such as a brisk 15-minute walk, to help you develop a practical exercise routine; then gradually increase the length or frequency of your sessions until you're ready for something more serious, such as working out in a gym or using an exercise machine at home. The advantage of walking is that it takes you places: try to build it into essential or useful journeys, choosing the long route to a destination whenever you can spare the time.

If you try to do too much too soon, you're likely to become discouraged or, worse, injure yourself. It's often a good idea to take a class or use a trainer to help you learn the correct way to exercise. Classes and trainers have the added advantage of providing social support and encouragement to help you stick with your program.

It doesn't really matter what kind of exercise you do, so long as it interests you, gets you moving, and is enjoyable enough for you to stick with it. In fact, you may choose a variety of activities so that you don't overuse certain muscles, or get bored and quit. Aerobic exercises are excellent if you want to improve your cardiovascular health (by getting your heart pumping at the target rate for your age and weight) or lose weight. Some classes are very active and have a strong social component. However, if your schedule won't accommodate regular classes, activities you can do on your own, such as cycling or running, will be better. Swimming is great for those who want an aerobic workout with low impact on their joints. Weight training can be tailored to meet several different fitness goals, including weight loss, muscle strengthening, and improving bone or joint health. Take advice from a trained professional and always carry out weight training under supervision.

If you keep your long-term goals in mind as you exercise, you'll be better prepared to deal with the inevitable times when motivation is hard to find. Surprisingly, losing weight isn't always the best motivator. It can be discouraging if you don't shed the pounds as quickly as you hoped. However, if you set yourself a range of goals (anything from a certain "distance" on the exercise bicycle to being able to keep up with your children without losing your breath), then you're more likely to stick with your regime.

Exercise is especially important if you're sedentary for most of the day. Try to go for a brisk walk at lunchtime, and whenever you're working at a desk have a good stretch every 15 minutes.

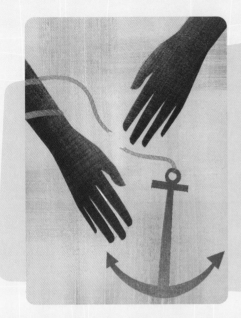

Exercise 17

Cut out
the excuses

We all recognize in theory the benefit of regular physical activity, but this doesn't stop us finding reasons not to exercise. I'm too old; I'd hurt myself; I'd look foolish; It takes too much time; I'm too fat ... . Each of these excuses serves to protect us from something we fear. We allow ourselves to avoid something that might be uncomfortable physically or socially. However, in the process we deny ourselves the countless benefits of exercise. If you can think of good reasons why you shouldn't exercise, take the following steps to find better reasons why you should.

1 Make two columns on a sheet of paper or in your journal. In the first column, write down every excuse you commonly use for not exercising.

2 In the second column, write down counter-arguments to your excuses. For example, if you think you're too old: "There are many people older than I am who exercise and are fit." If you think

you'd look silly: "My aim is to get fit, not to take part in a fashion show."

3 Visualize yourself as someone who shamefully avoids what they know is good – indeed, necessary – for them.

4 Pick an activity and just start it. Action is sometimes the only way to end an inner dialogue of endless prevarications.

Pampering yourself

At times it's good to take serious measures to look after yourself in ways that go above and beyond the basics of monitoring your health, eating and sleeping well, and exercising regularly. By stretching self-maintenance to the point of luxury, you can replenish your depleted energy and enthusiasm – and have an enjoyable time in the process.

CREATING A HOME SPA

Few experiences are more relaxing or revitalizing than spending a day in a spa. However, for most of us it's not practical to go on regular spa getaways or to re-fit our bathrooms with specialist equipment. Fortunately, there are some simple and inexpensive ways to recreate the spa effect in your own home.

It's not so much the range of treatments available that makes a spa enjoyable and refreshing, but the feeling that you're retreating from everyday concerns and taking special care of yourself. So it's important to create a spa mentality. Make an appointment for your day of well-being. Arrange to have the house to yourself – let someone else take care of the children for the day. Stock up in advance on products that you enjoy using, such as foot massage lotion, a facial scrub, deep moisturizers, bath salts, natural aromatic oils and scented candles.

When the day comes, unplug the phone and switch off the TV and radio. Turn down the lighting and put on some soothing music. Have warm, soft towels ready to dry yourself after your bath and shower. Read, garden, meditate. Cook delicious, healthy meals. What matters is that you do simple, healthy things that make you happy.

Therapeutic massage, aromatherapy, and beauty or grooming treatments can all enhance well-being. Massage releases tensions, relieves any muscle pain, improves circulation and can ease headaches. Aromatherapy, whether self-administered or practiced professionally, can have a marked effect on your mood and your ability to concentrate. Essential oils massaged into the body (diluted in a carrier oil) or burned in an oil burner have well-proven properties: for example, choose lavender, neroli, ylang-ylang or chamomile for their calming, anti-depressant effects, jasmine for post-natal depression. Esthetic treatments such as facials, manicures and pedicures will help you feel more presentable and energized.

Pampering yourself can seem somewhat hedonistic, but remember that these therapies can have a positive impact on your emotional and physical health. Think how much better you perform both at work and at home when you're alert, relaxed and free of discomfort.

Although women are more likely to explore these techniques, there's no reason why men shouldn't use them too. Indulge yourself once a month if you can. You've probably earned it.

Good night

Many people don't get as much sleep as they need in order to function at their best. We're so busy that sleeping can sometimes seem like a waste of valuable time. However, restful sleep helps your body to fend off illness and recover from stress. Your mind needs sleep as well. You deal with so much sensory input throughout your waking hours that your mind needs time off to download images, memories and tasks. A well-rested person is able to concentrate better, think more creatively, and solve problems better than a tired person. When you're chronically sleep-deprived, you're more likely to make poor decisions, agree to

things that you later regret, snap at people out of irritation and take longer than normal to get things done. Fatigue also contributes to a significant number of accidents – on the road, at work and at home.

Poor sleep frequently results from problems in your life that remain unresolved and distressing at the end of the day. There are

MAKE YOUR BEDROOM RESTFUL

Your sleep will be more restful if your sleeping environment is conducive to resting. Here are some tips to help to make your bedroom as sleep-inducing as possible.

- Choose calming colors for your bedroom décor: light blues and greens or soft pinks. Ensure that your lighting is soft and adjustable.

- Set a temperature that is conducive to sleeping – typically about 62°F (16°C).

- Use light- and sound-blocking shades and curtains on your windows.

- Change the bed linens regularly. Pollen and dust collect in your bedclothes, and fresh linens just smell and feel better.

- Burn lavender oil to help to create a relaxing mood.

- Reduce the clutter. Clutter sends the message to your brain that you have unfinished business to take care of, which makes it harder to relax. For the same reason don't leave work in the bedroom (and never work in bed).

- Invest in a good, firm mattress. Your sleep will improve dramatically when your body is well supported. You'll toss and turn less if you're comfortable.

several steps you can take to clear your mind of such worries. One of the best is to recall today's accomplishments and plan tomorrow. Make notes on both in your journal. When you close the journal, close your mind to all these concerns. If anxious thoughts continue to pop into your head, acknowledge them by saying to yourself: "Yes, this is important. I'll deal with it tomorrow." Then take some time to prepare your mind and body for a restful night's sleep (see exercise, opposite). If, when you review your day, you're able to acknowledge that you lived it in accordance with your priorities and values, you're more likely to have an untroubled night.

It's well known that coffee or tea before bedtime are sleep thieves that disrupt body rhythms. Less familiar is the fact that coffee remains in the body for several hours, and up to five times longer if you're pregnant. Confine your coffee-drinking to mornings if you can bear to.

The exercise opposite outlines a sensible pre-sleep routine. If you're unable to get a good night's sleep despite taking these steps, you may need to seek advice from a sleep specialist.

There has been much debate on the merits of napping during the day. In fact, this is a perfectly sensible way to catch up on lost sleep or to unwind after a burst of energetic activity. You should bear in mind, however, that you won't awaken to the point of full "performance efficiency" for up to 20 minutes after coming out of the nap.

Develop a pre-bedtime routine

Regular bedtime routines signal to your body and mind that sleep will shortly follow. The following suggested procedure is a workable starting-point for experiment.

1   Go to bed at roughly the same time every night. Forcing yourself to go to bed early or staying up later than normal can disrupt your body's natural rhythms.

2   Have a small tryptophan-rich snack or drink, such as yogurt or milk, about an hour before bedtime. Tryptophan is an amino acid which the body converts into serotonin, a sleep-inducing neurotransmitter. Eat your last big meal at least three hours before bedtime (digestion increases body temperature, which makes it harder to get to sleep). Avoid caffeine after supper, but have a cup of chamomile tea late in the evening for its calming effect.

3   Turn off the TV at least 30 minutes before bedtime. Put on some relaxing instrumental music instead.

4   If you read at bedtime, choose reading material that won't keep you awake. Poetry or short stories may be better than an "unputdownable" thriller.

5   Do some gentle stretching exercises. Spend a few minutes taking deep breaths to calm your body.

6   Turn off the lights and allow sleep to descend. If it doesn't come immediately, be patient: worry is counter-productive.

Just you

Some readers may have difficulty accepting some of the precepts in this chapter because they might seem to border on the "selfish". But is it really selfish to be passionately dedicated to maximizing one's full potential for inner peace and the happiness that springs from this? You are the biggest investment you'll ever have to manage. If you don't take excellent care of yourself, that investment will pay poorly in dividends all through your life. So it's not a matter of acting selfishly, but of responsible self-management. By coming to a balanced relationship with your inner self, mentally and spiritually, you're showing true respect for the gift of human life. And the benefits of this will spread to all the people around you – family, friends, acquaintances. You'll be for them a source of wisdom, strength, understanding and – hopefully – inspiration.

Why are you here?

Some people get on with their lives without ever feeling the need to look outside themselves and wonder where they are going, or what the purpose of everything might be. The day-to-day business of living, with all its worries and strivings, completely fills their minds. When problems arise, they resolve them as best they can, improvising with various degrees of anxiety or panic, without ever feeling the need to question why such problems have arisen in the first place, or whether there is a "place", inside oneself perhaps, where such problems don't arise – or don't cause such emotional turmoil.

Others, however, are conscious that something seems to be missing from their lives, even though they might not know quite what it is. They have a sense that there's something they could have achieved or experienced. Often it's the burden of endless routine – periods of drudgery, alternating with household chores, punctuated by all-too-rare passages of genuine pleasure or stimulation. For others, it's the absence of a special perspective, maybe a spiritual perspective, that would give life depth or meaning. Where meaning is missing, the void is often filled by boredom, inertia, hopelessness, fear – even despair.

At the other end of the spectrum are people who *have* discovered that special ingredient, or at least have glimpsed it well enough to give them a guiding star to live by. They believe that being alive brings with it both privilege and purpose. Life is rich and endlessly bountiful. If they have not yet discovered their own particular purpose, they at least know where to look. Like anyone else, they are subject to change, chance, ill health, the loss of physical powers with age, and bereavement. But somehow there's a spirit inside them that gives them strength and resourcefulness in misfortune. They meet challenges with resolve and even excitement. They are actively engaged in life and look for ways to live out their destiny.

When you lack a sense of meaning or purpose in life, it's like standing on the edge of a canyon and not knowing how to get to the other side. But the question arises, Is it really on the other side of the canyon that all the answers lie? To tackle a sense of emptiness in life, the first step is to see whether the redress can be found close at hand, in your immediate circumstances, your character, yourself. Could it be that you're excluded, not from an inaccessible world of meaning, the unpromised land on the other side of the canyon, but from the key that will unlock for you all the possibilities to be found on this side of the canyon? Perhaps the solutions are closer than you think.

As a starting-point, try to identify the nature of your frustration, and see whether that suggests a direction to explore. Some people are acutely aware of being unable to express through everyday channels what they really think or feel. Others fail to find emotional connection in their relationships. Others again feel that their intellects rust unused while their thinking has nothing to concentrate on but trivia. And, of course, there are those whose problem is that the demands of parenting or a career, or both, allow no time for themselves; while for others the role of parent or businessperson is the solution, not the problem.

Creativity, love, career, enterprise, intellectual engagement and spiritual practices of various kinds are all valid routes to a sense of purpose, but there is no one-size-fits-all formula. The only generalization that can be offered is that meaning comes from a true acceptance of yourself and a pride in your uniqueness. Find yourself and be yourself.

Exercise 19

Find signposts to meaning

To find true meaning in your life requires that you develop an appreciation for the many things that make you unique – your beliefs, your values, your talents, your interests, your relationships, and your appreciation of the world around you.

1   In a notebook, list your accomplishments so far – not only educational and professional, but also personal projects, such as building a relationship or a home, or bringing up children.

2   Write down the main sources of your dissatisfaction or frustration. What needs do you have that your current life is preventing you from satisfying? Assess the importance of these needs.

3   List the "big" questions you have and any tentative answers that you've discovered so far. Write down any reservations you have about these possible answers.

4   Identify the things currently in your life that give you the greatest sense of satisfaction and fulfillment.

5   Write down your values and beliefs, and analyze how they inform each of the main aspects of your life.

6   List your special talents, including life skills such as communication.

7   Now read what you've written, and use these notes as the basis for a tentative mission statement on where you are currently finding purpose and where you plan to find purpose in the future.

Finding the real you

Our destiny is not a solo voyage. Our lives are so bound up with a multitude of rules and conventions, spoken and unspoken, that it could be said that we pipe to other people's tunes as much as to our own. This is nothing to complain about, as societies all need their rules if people are to rub along together with a mutual understanding of what is acceptable and what is not. Then again, we enter various relationships, many of them voluntary, many of them not, or not exactly; and these are workable only if agreed guidelines are followed. This applies to the relations between partners, parents and children, employers and employees, and indeed every other sphere of life in which humans

interact with each other. Conventions, obligations, responsibilities abound. And with them come various roles we have to play, switching from one to another at different times – for example, from parent in the morning, to manager during the working day, to dinner host or guest in the evening. Sometimes these roles involve dealing with pressures, and to carry them out successfully we have to suppress some of our true feelings, refrain from speaking aloud some of our thoughts, and conform instead with a prescribed set of responses to a range of different situations. No wonder that some people begin to feel at times that they're in danger of losing their true selves.

A balanced life is inevitably going to involve some social role play – unless you choose to live as a hermit. You'll have to behave and speak in a certain way just as you have to dress in a certain way. To say that this compromises your individuality is to display insecurity, because in reality your role and your self are distinct from each other, even though they may be closely related. (How closely depends on the role itself. For example, you might feel that being a parent is a large part of who you are, whereas you're unlikely to feel this way about being an applicant for a bank loan.)

If you're uncomfortable about playing a role, various possible factors could be at work. You might simply find the role difficult – it takes practice to be good at making a speech, or at being entertaining in polite company. Or it could be that the role is in some way contrary to your intuitive sense of rightness, which might be so if it involves lying, or being unkind or inflexible. In the first case, you need to accept that practice will make you better, and regard your learning as a challenge. In the second case, you need to ask how important the offended values are, and whether you should quit the role or, alternatively, find a way to reconcile the opposites – which, after all, is what we often do in life generally (for example, we might have to take a hard line with someone, while at the same time being sympathetic to them).

It's worth bearing in mind that even within social roles there's usually scope to express your personality. If you feel that you are *acting* the part of teacher, or salesperson, or middle manager, why not see what would happen if you allowed more of yourself to show through? Make the most of work-related social opportunities to unwind and be yourself, so that your colleagues really get to know you.

Parents in particular often feel that they have no time to be themselves. One approach to this problem is to cultivate pride in the universally acknowledged gift of parental sacrifice – an honorable tradition – while being inventive in looking for opportunities for personal fulfillment. As with any difficulty over roles, the important thing to remember is that your inner self, with its creative inner life of thoughts and feelings, is yours alone. It need never experience defeat.

Exercise 20

Dream-catching

People daydream all the time, mostly on automatic pilot. Some of your ideas are simply brilliant and you don't even realize it. How often do you have a great thought and then rack your brain for days trying to remember it? Probably every day.

1   Carry a little notebook for writing down any quirky ideas, thoughts or phrases you feel are worth preserving – perhaps because they express something individual about you. Don't worry about neatness – the idea is to express your inner life, and there's no need for the notebook to be tidy, unless you particularly want it to be.

2   Record your dreams in the notebook too, if you can remember them. The idea is to build up a random record of your inner life, and your dreams will be gone forever unless you write them down.

3   Use metaphor and simile to record your experiences. For example, if you've seen someone whose stiff, humorless posturing reminds you of a comic character, jot this down before you forget it.

4   Write down the thoughts you have after seeing films or plays, or listening to music. These experiences can be some of the richest in all your inner life, and it would be a pity to lose them.

5   Don't censor your ideas – just write what you think. But make sure the notebook doesn't fall into the wrong hands!

Nourishing your mind

The mind is like the body in one important respect: it needs exercise to keep it in shape. Although we all think all the time, that does not mean that our mind is enjoying a healthy workout or being stimulated to any real degree. Even at work, we may often find ourselves acting on automatic pilot, our routine being so ingrained in us that we go through the motions of thinking without full mental engagement. There are times for dreaming, as we have seen. But there are also times when we would benefit from using our reasoning powers and critical faculties,

ENGAGING WITH PHILOSOPHY

Philosophy was once widely believed to be pointless intellectual hair-splitting, but over the past five years or so it has regained something of a popular following. Any published philosopher is likely to provide a stimulating intellectual challenge to any moderately well-educated reader. The advantage of well-argued philosophy for anyone in search of mental stimulation is that it requires little specialized knowledge (it does use a few special terms, such as dualism – the belief that mind and body are different kinds of entity). Philosophy is the application of the rational mind to questions of universal significance: What is experience? What is the mind? How do we acquire knowledge? How reliable are our perceptions and deductions? What is truth? How should human beings behave? The latter question, in the realm of ethics, has acquired new relevance in relation to the rights and wrongs of cloning. A good book to start with, although slightly out of date, is Bertrand Russell's *The Problems of Philosophy* (1912).

giving 100 per cent of our attention to something that is mentally challenging, instead of allowing our thoughts to drift distractedly.

One of the enemies of intellectual sharpness is the least demanding form of passive entertainment we see on TV. This may offer a good way to relax after a hard working day, but many people use it as their main recreation. Meanwhile, reading tends to be neglected, despite the popularity of blockbusters. Reading works of literary fiction and discussing their merits with friends, or in a reading group established for the purpose, is an excellent way to stretch the intellect's capacities, for there is nothing better for the mind than making reasoned judgments and arguing a convincing case for them. A purer form of intellectual stimulation can be found in cerebral games such as chess and mah-jong.

Unleashing your creativity

Creativity is a state of mind rather than a set of skills. It's an imaginative involvement in the process of making something, even something that's fleeting or intangible. And this, of course, means that we're all creative, or can be, even if we have no interest in painting, writing or any other kind of traditional craft. Whenever you solve a problem, look at a situation from a different perspective, use something in a new way, or stage an event, you're being creative. You're applying the resourcefulness of the imagination. There's infinite scope for creativity in all aspects of life – home, relationships, work, leisure. Common creative

activities include parenting (which involves storytelling and improvising in various ways, especially when explaining the origins of things), gardening, homemaking, cooking, letter writing, entertaining guests, and even choosing your clothes for the day.

The advantage of creativity is that it provides a channel for making a positive contribution to the world that expresses some aspect of yourself – not necessarily an expression of feeling (though it can indeed be this) but an expression, let's say, of energy. To be creative you sometimes just have to let go – which is healthy for people sometimes. People who don't try something they are interested in are usually inhibited in some way (such as lack of confidence), though it can also be lack of time or money. Don't think of exploring your creativity as an indulgence. It's a possible route to an enormously enriched sense of well-being. The converse of this is that the creative impulse, if thwarted, causes frustration, which you may not even be able to diagnose. If you do feel an ill-defined sense of being blocked in some way, why not try a creative activity to see if it brings you any release?

The first thing you'll need to do is choose a suitable avenue. Do you tend to think in words or pictures? If the former, you could try writing; if the latter, maybe one of the visual arts would be more appropriate. Are you solitary by nature or gregarious? Whatever activity you choose there'll usually be a group, class or workshop you can join, though many pursuits – especially writing and art – can be profitably pursued solo, or with just a teacher. Right from the outset you'll need to overcome fear of failure, and this too is one of the healthy aspects of creativity. It's good for you to be a complete beginner, just as you were in your schooldays – making mistakes, even embarrassing ones, and maybe being bottom of the class. Successful creative work often emerges after a long history of false starts and wrong turnings.

If art or design is your chosen subject, don't be afraid to doodle. Or, if you're trying your hand at writing, you can doodle with words. Just seeing what happens is an important part of being creative. You'll make discoveries that you'd never have arrived at by a more formal method of working.

Most creative people are fascinated not only by the project they're working on but also by the way in which their imagination operates – the decisions they find themselves making, for reasons that perhaps have little to do with rational logic. It can be illuminating to keep a journal of your creative work – with sketches, jottings, and notes on anything you see, hear or feel that inspires you. As you begin to be attuned to your chosen medium, you'll become alert to what other people say about it, especially if they're practitioners themselves, and so you might decide to write in your journal any memorable observations you come across.

Exercise 21

Enter the creative Zone

Many artists in different media describe entering the "Zone" – a heightened mental state in which the mind is so absorbed in its imaginative project that it pays no attention to any other stimuli for anything up to an hour or so. When you come out of the Zone you look back at what you've created with surprise: only now do you realize how absorbed you've been, how quickly time has passed. And you can experience your project like an outsider, as if someone else has been working on it. If you're a writer, say, you can enjoy your writing as if you were a reader coming to it for the first time. Here are four tips on creating the right circumstances for entering the Zone.

1   Choose a environment with a quiet ambience. Turn off your cell phone, and make sure that you have all your materials and equipment ready.

2   Make sure that you have plenty of time, so that you finish only when you feel that you've completed a satisfactory phase of the work.

3   Eat well before you start. If it's in the morning, have a good breakfast. Hunger can throw the creative impulse off course, not least because you'll have to break off to eat something.

4   Don't be self-conscious, waiting for yourself to be aware of entering the Zone. Just work away and absorb yourself.

Taking an interest in the world

Sometimes you may feel you don't have time to take an interest in the world outside the confines of your own life. Or you might feel there's so much going on "out there" that there's no point in even trying to keep up with the news – this can certainly be a problem in an age of media frenzy and multi-channel TV. Or you might feel disillusioned about the way in which the world, or your own society, is conducting itself and feel inclined to disengage. It would be a pity if any of these attitudes prevented you from exploring what's happening around you.

To maintain a healthy life balance, it's good to be able to place your own special concerns in a wider perspective – not least because this is

a way of understanding how fortunate you are. You're at the center of a set of concentric circles – family, neighborhood, community, region, country, culture. Your life encompasses, and is impacted by, the outer circles, not just the inner. And within these outer circles there's great richness as well as great suffering and injustice.

Keeping in touch with the world enhances your individuality, because you'll inevitably choose to be selective, in line with what interests you. Anyone who doesn't read the papers or watch or listen to the news, at least occasionally, is missing out. But there's more to the world than current affairs. History enables us to see how we are the product of evolving circumstances, often incorporating an element of conflict. Nature gives us plenty to wonder at and make us question how it can be that life-forms are so incredibly varied. Travel brings us into contact with other ways of living – the people who get the most out of it are certainly those who interact with the people and the culture.

It's pleasurable to share such discoveries with children. But even if you haven't any kids, you can enjoy, alone or with friends or a partner, the great adventure of learning about the world you live in. Limiting your horizons to personal matters can be dangerous – it keeps you within your box. Staying connected with some of life's many manifestations, at home and abroad, in the present and the past, and even tracking projections about the future, is endlessly enriching.

One step deeper

At the beginning of this chapter we listed, among the "big" questions, What does it all mean? It's possible for us to go through all our years without seriously addressing this question. On the other hand, if you're in the process of straightening out the kinks in your life, there would be one kink left if you didn't pay some attention to your spiritual beliefs. Essentially, this means working out your view of what lies beyond ourselves and how this view might equip you to deal with serious misfortune, bereavement, and the inevitability of your own demise.

It's outside the remit of this book to offer possible answers on this question, but it's worth making two observations. Firstly, there are profound truths in all religions, and the ecumenical movement, which seeks a synthesis of faiths, is a positive development. Secondly, many people these days look to the East for their sense of spiritual meaning – especially to Buddhism (including Zen) and Taoism. Cynics might argue that it's wrong to choose a set of beliefs as if you were choosing goods from a catalog, on the grounds that beliefs make sense only within the culture you're brought up in. But actually many of the world's problems stem from unshakable convictions that are rooted in culture. And to take your bearings from the East is to view your life from a refreshingly different perspective.

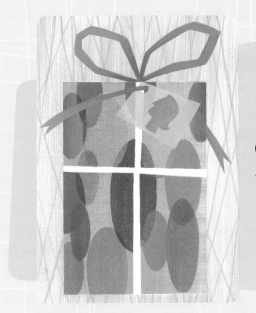

Give yourself time to think

It's good to allow your reason or your intuition, or both, to give you an approximate picture of what you truly believe; or to find a spiritual practice that brings harmony between your body, mind and spirit. There's no need to be too concerned if your view of the spirit is vague. The first stage in spiritual enlightenment is to spend some time among beneficial influences. Below are suggestions for achieving this.

1 Spend some time alone – perhaps when the children have gone to bed, or are in summer camp. Try to spend a whole day alone in a quiet place where you can be inspired by the beauty of nature.

2 Try meditation, or just sitting quietly with your eyes closed listening to gentle sounds and allowing your thoughts to pass across your mind like clouds.

3 Go on a retreat, perhaps combining it with a healthy-eating or detox regime.

4 Read some classic texts of spirituality, such as the *Tao Te Ching*, which teaches that we should bend to the rhythms of nature rather than resisting change and attempting to impose our will upon everything.

5 Listen to sacred music, such as Gregorian chant or Indian ragas. Let its spiritual beauty permeate your thoughts.

6 Talk to people about their spiritual experiences and beliefs. Find out where others find life's meaning.

Conclusion

Balance is a choice. It doesn't happen by itself, nor should it be taken for granted. Balance only occurs if you *make* it happen. So many things in life are beyond our control, but we spend a lot of time trying to control them anyway. Living a balanced life is not about being in control of all things, but rather, about managing those things over which we *do* have an influence and managing our reaction to everything else. Often we get so bogged down worrying about what we *can't* do that we overlook what we *can* do. The main intention behind this book has been to awaken in you the realization that you have immense power to shape your life in a way that will bring you satisfaction. Indeed, you should treat it as a responsibility to yourself to do just that.

Life is constantly evolving. Nevertheless, many of us like stability and resist change – particularly sudden, radical change. Routines promote a sense of security: knowing more or less what's coming next can be comforting. As a result, when we're faced with a decision about whether to stay in our current situation or move on (for example, if we're offered a new job), the temptation to stay put in familiar surroundings can be hard to resist. To make it easier to break the surface tension, list the positive and negative aspects of any move you might be considering. If the benefits outweigh the drawbacks, your motivation

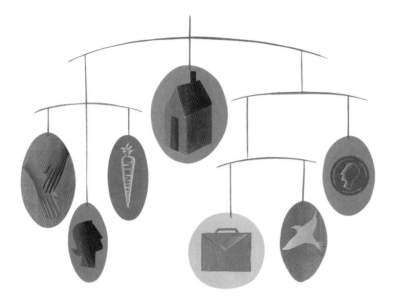

to accept – and, indeed, to embrace – the change will increase greatly. Ask for help from the people you're closest to – call on their support through the change process and make sure you recognize and reward both your efforts and theirs. We urge you to actively seek out productive change within your life. This is by far the most effective way to achieve the balance that you desire.

Throughout this book, we've touched on the important aspects of balance. You've been given the tools with which you can fashion a life that will work well for you. We hope that you've been inspired to grapple with the challenges you face. We've encouraged you to consider some of the concerns that may hinder your progress and provided exercises designed to motivate and guide you to take action toward balancing your life. There's no right or wrong way of going about it: each of us faces a unique set of circumstances. It's for you to determine the specific steps that are best for you.

You should now have a clear idea of the values that are most important to you and that influence your choices. Make choices that are true to your ideals. Part of what makes it so difficult to achieve satisfaction in life is that we go about attempting to please everyone but ourselves. For example, the son or daughter who enters the career nominated by their parents instead of the one they prefer, or the person who always says yes to a friend's requests, for fear of causing offence – even when they're being asked to do something they'd rather not do, or haven't got time to do. On the other hand, when your choices are guided by the precepts that you hold most dear, you're much more

likely to be pleased with the results, and so will the other people in your life.

People resist looking too far ahead, because they believe that they're powerless to control or foretell what will happen in the future: they see no point in making plans. However, the purpose of planning is not to exert absolute control over what will happen, but to maximize the possibility of achieving productive, positive outcomes. We shouldn't attempt to manipulate the future, as a puppeteer does a puppet, rather, we should be alert to the opportunities that beckon and go out to seize them with vigor, enthusiasm and an expectation of success. A powerfully compelling vision for your life can propel you forward like the wind that fills the sails of a ship. The task is not to control the wind, but to direct the movements of the ship so that it stays on course. Many people have no destination in mind and therefore it's little wonder that they don't feel that they're going anywhere. To live a balanced life, you must see a future for yourself that is truly inspiring and moves you forward.

As the world around you changes, so do you. This means that any plans you formulate may need to change, too (see box, p.154). Likely, the fundamental elements, such as your key values and ideals, will remain stable over time, but your goals and priorities will evolve as new twists and turns occur in your life. As aspects of your life change, such as your career, health and family, what's most important to you will change accordingly. Despite this, we frequently stick to a plan or a choice even when it should be clear that it no longer makes sense to do so. That's part of being creatures of habit and being resistant to change. We may even think that to change our mind would be weak. However, the strongest, most enlightened people tend to be the most flexible. There are many good reasons for revising, or even reversing, a decision. Perhaps, as is so often the case, you made a decision without being in possession of all the relevant facts: it would be foolish not to act on a later piece of information that, had you known it at the time, would have led you along a different path. For example, you join a new

MAP-READING

Bringing balance to your life is an ongoing process. You'll find it easier to achieve if you monitor your progress both in the short term and the long. Use the following strategies to refine your plans, goals and priorities in a clear-headed way.

- Develop the habit of making an entry in your journal (see pp.30–31) at the end of each day without fail. Record each day's accomplishments and prepare yourself for the challenges of the next day.
- Periodically review your notes on the exercises in the book (especially those in the first chapter) and assess whether they still apply. Refine your notes if necessary.
- Repeat the "Take your life for a spin" exercise (see p.29) now and on a regular basis – perhaps every six months.
- Look at each area of your life and identify what's going well. Think of ways to apply these positives to other areas.
- Review your goals and plans in any areas that are falling short of your expectations. Brainstorm five to ten ideas for improving your progress in these areas. Write them down and leave them for several days. Then pick the best idea, turn it into a goal and develop a plan of action.

company because you're promised a certain job specification that appeals to you. Several years on, it becomes clear to you that the role that had attracted you to the organization doesn't exist. There's no shame in cutting your losses and moving to a job that better meets your needs. And you'll find that your life experience is enriched even by your "wrong" turnings.

You'll be far more successful in achieving balance if you're open to any possibility, willing to follow your intuition and determined to find ways to develop your abilities to the full. Give up old routines that you've outgrown – otherwise they clutter up your time just as old clothes in a closet clutter up your space. And don't wait until you're certain you'll succeed before you decide to try new things: fear of failure is hardly a worthwhile motivator. It's far better to make a mistake, and so find out for sure that something won't work, than to wonder "what might have been" for the rest of your life. There's no rule that you have to get it right the first time – each attempt you make helps you to shape the next. The harder we have to work to meet our goals, the sweeter it is when we achieve them.

Achieving balance won't always be easy, but it's certainly well worth the effort. We hope that you'll achieve the life of your aspirations and lead it with great satisfaction and fulfillment. It's yours to create and live.

Further reading

Capacchione, L.
Visioning: Ten Steps to Designing the Life of Your Dreams, J. P. Tarcher (New York), 2000

Cooper, R. K.
The Other 90%: How to Unlock Your Vast Untapped Potential for Leadership and Life, Three Rivers Press (New York), 2002

Covey, S. R.
The Seven Habits of Highly Effective People, Simon & Schuster (New York), 1990

Eisenson, M., et al.
Invest in Yourself, John Wiley & Sons (New York), 1998

Ellis, D.
Creating Your Future, Houghton Mifflin Company (New York), 1998

Fortgang, L. B.
Living Your Best Life, J. P. Tarcher (New York)/HarperCollins (London), 2001

Fortgang, L. B.
Take Yourself to the Top, Warner Books (New York), 1998

Frankel, L. P.
Jump-Start Your Career, Three Rivers Press (New York), 1998

Gerrish, M.
The Mind-Body Makeover Project, Contemporary Books (Chicago), 2003

Greene, B.
The Get with the Program! Guide to Good Eating, Simon & Schuster (New York), 2003

Harris, C.
Minimize Stress, Maximize Success, Chronicle Books (San Francisco)/ Duncan Baird (London), 2003

Idzikowski, C.
Learn to Sleep Well, Chronicle Books (San Francisco)/Duncan Baird (London), 2000

Leider, R. J.
The Power of Purpose, Berrett-Koehler (San Francisco), 1997

Morgenstern, J.
Time Management from the Inside Out, Henry Holt & Company (New York)/Hodder & Stoughton General (London), 2000

Mulligan, E.
Life Coaching for Work, Piatkus Books (London), 2000

Pegrum, J.
Peace at Home, Chronicle Books (San Francisco)/ *At Peace at Home*, Duncan Baird (London), 2003

Richardson, C.
Life Makeovers, Broadway Books (New York), 2000

Richardson, C.
Take Time for Your Life, Broadway Books (New York), 1998

Smith, K.
Kathy Smith's Getting Better All the Time, Warner Books (New York), 1999

White, J.
Work Less, Make More, John Wiley & Sons (New York), 1999

Index

Acknowledgments

We wish to thank our parents, Francis and Patricia Hinz and James and Ann Giglio, our other family, and our friends, who have all shaped, encouraged, inspired and supported us through the years. Our lives have been greatly enriched in so many ways by so many people through their words of wisdom, their example and experiences: to each of you we offer our heartfelt thanks.

Also, we sincerely appreciate the readers of this book, who will continue to make these words come alive by applying them to their own lives and by helping others to live more balanced lives.

Contact the authors

To receive a weekly e-mail newsletter or to learn more about Michael and Jessica's Life Balance Coaching services, visit their website at www.hinzdocs.com or e-mail them at Coach@HinzDocs.com.